With Latin in the Service of the Popes

Antonio Cardinal Bacci with the newly published fourth edition of his *Italian-Latin Dictionary*, August 23, 1963

With Latin in the Service of the Popes
The Memoirs of Antonio Cardinal Bacci (1885-1971)

ENGLISH TRANSLATION OF
*CON IL LATINO A SERVIZIO
DI QUATTRO PAPI*

Translated by
DR. ANTHONY LO BELLO

Original Italian Edition 1964,
Con il Latino a Servizio di Quattro Papi
© Editrice Studium (Rome)

2020 © by Arouca Press
Newly Revised and Typeset
English translation & Foreword © Anthony Lo Bello

Photo of Cardinal Bacci used with permission from Getty Images

Every effort has been made to contact the original copyright holder, Marsilio Bacci, for direct permission for this new edition. Several direct relatives of the author have been contacted who have given their explicit permission to have this edition published. No copyright infringement is intended.

All rights reserved:
No part of this book may be reproduced or transmitted,
in any form or by any means, without permission

ISBN: 978-1-7770523-9-3 (pbk)
ISBN: 978-1-989905-00-5 (hardcover)

Arouca Press
PO Box 55003
Bridgeport PO
Waterloo, ON N2J3G0
Canada
www.aroucapress.com
Send inquiries to info@aroucapress.com

DEDICATION

To the memory of
A. Cardinal Galli
and Msgr. N. Sebastiani,
distinguished Latinists,
who, by their teaching and writing,
led me to the study and love of the Latin language

CONTENTS

Letters of Acknowledgment to the Translator xiii
Foreword xv
Introduction xix

I. From Florence to Rome 1
  1. Life with the Seminarians 1
  2. The Order to Leave for Rome 2
  3. My First Meeting with Msgr. Montini 4

II. In the Service of Pius XI (1922-1939) 9
  1. My First Experience with Latin in the Curia 9
  2. A Bad Mistake in Latin 11
  3. "I've Been Waiting for Msgr. Bacci for an Hour!" 15
  4. A Monument to Garibaldi and One in
     Commemoration of Vatican I 19
  5. Pius XI at the End 25
     Pius XI Pont. Max. 30
     Pius XI. Supreme Pontiff 32

III. In the Service of Pius XII (1939-1958) 35
  1. The Best Prepared through Wisdom and Divine Grace . . 35
  2. The War 38
  3. Pius XII Encourages Me to Write the
     Italian-Latin Dictionary of Modern Words 43
  4. The Last Days of Pius XII 47
     Pius XII Pont. Max. 48
     Pius XII, Supreme Pontiff 50

IV. In the Service of John XXIII 55
  1. A Meeting with Msgr. Roncalli 55
  2. Good Pope John 56
  3. Pontifical Speeches and Documents 58
  4. The Second Vatican Council 60
  5. A Bed That Is an Altar 61

V. In The Service of Paul VI 63
   1. *Habemus Papam!* 63
   2. The Continuation of the Council 64
   3. The Goodness and Friendliness of the Pontiff 65
   4. The Trip to Palestine 66

VI. Latin and the Council 67
   1. What Language is Used at the Council,
      and in What Style of Latin Are the
      Conciliar Documents and Acts Written? 67
        The Constitution *Veterum Sapientia* 67
        The Views of Fr. Dehon 67
        Linguistic Organization of the Council 69
   2. In Which Language? 70
        A Plain and Scholastic Latin 72
        Keep to the Roman Pronunciation. 73
   3. In Which Latin? 75
        Humanistic Latin and a Dignified
        and Decorous Latin 75

VII. Latin and Esperanto 79
   1. Can Latin Really Become an International Language? .. 79
   2. Esperanto 82
        Two Necessary Steps 83
        The Example of the Church. 84

VIII. The Latin Language Alive in the World 87
   1. Latin in the School 87
        Latin—Yes!, Latin—No!, Latin—How? 87
   2. The Development of Latin into Its Classical, Patristic,
      Mediaeval and Modern Forms. 89
        Christian Latin. 91
        The Humanists 93
        The Work and the Influence of the Church 94
        The Humanists and the Church 96
        The Principles of the Church in Her Use of Latin ... 101
        A Constitution on Latin. 102

    The Debate about Latin 103
    The Reasons for the Decline in the Study of Latin . . . 106

Conclusion 110
Index. 113
About the Translator 117

LETTERS OF ACKNOWLEDGEMENT
to the Translator from Professor Marsilio Bacci, Nephew of Cardinal Bacci

I.

Prof. Marsilio Bacci
Via Bondi, 3
40138 Bologna

March 2, 1989

Dear Professor Lo Bello,
    I am very grateful for your interest in the work of my uncle, the late Antonio Cardinal Bacci.
    Editrice Studium was right in telling you to apply to me because in his testament, the Cardinal made me the heir of all his publications, for he wanted to acknowledge in this way both my collaboration and my work as executor of his will.
    While reserving the rights that are mine by his will, I am happy to grant you permission to translate and to publish in English the book *Con il latino a servizio di quattro Papi.*
    Alas, even his well-known *Italian-Latin Dictionary of Modern and Difficult-to-Translate Words* is no longer in print, even though the fifth edition, to which I contributed a small part was ready for the press. I could do no more than write a memorial for my uncle in the March, 1981 issue of *Latinitas* and add a list of the last Italian words translated and diligently collated by me. This was to be my little tribute of acknowledgement to him who was a father to me, an orphan. And that was the only commemoration of him, as far as I know, on the occasion of the tenth anniversary of his death.
    For this reason, it pleases me greatly that America has not forgotten and does not want to forget him who enriched the Catholic Church with a Latin patrimony that cannot be renounced!

And, as a sign of this gratitude, I am sending you, dear Professor, my most cordial greetings.

Yours truly,
Marsilio Bacci

(translated from the Italian)

II.

Marsilius Antonio s. p. d.

Multas per gentes, multa per aequora vectus . . . aestiva otia consumpsi; nunc demum, ad optatam domum reversus, tuas gratissimas litteras inveni atque una commentariolum, in quo initium mei patrui operis in Anglorum sermonem a te conversum summa exspectatione ac prope attonitus perlegi.

Sermo enim, quo usus es, tam facilis et promptus et profluens est ut nativus, non ab alia lingua translatus, videatur.

Qua de re tibi maxime gratulor atque omnia bona faustaque opto. Vale.

Bononiae, a.d. III Id. Sept.

* * *

Marsilio to Anthony, Greetings!

Having travelled through many countries and over many seas . . . I have come to the end of my summer vacation; now at last, having returned to my dear home, I have found your most welcome letter waiting together with the journal, and I was astonished when I read through the first installment of your English translation of my uncle's book.

For your style is so easy to read, natural and fluid that one would think that one was reading the original work and not merely a translation.

I send you my heartiest congratulations for this accomplishment, along with all my best wishes.

Bologna
September 11, 1989

FOREWORD

It is wonderful that after fifty-six years, the valuable little book of Antonio Cardinal Bacci once again appears in print, this time in the English language. The translation is a private one that I made thirty years ago with the permission and approval of the Cardinal's nephew and heir, Professor Marsilio Bacci. At that time I was convinced, as I still am, that the reminiscences of a scholar of the first rank at the end of a productive career are both instructive and edifying for all people. His story has the additional tragic element that he lived to see the all but complete overthrow of Latin set in motion by the government of the Church which he had served as its chief Latinist for most of his learned life.

Antonio Bacci (1885–1971), at the time superior of the archdiocesan seminary in Florence, was summoned to Rome in 1922 to serve as a Latinist in the Secretariat of State, a position for which he was considered ideal by his superior, Alfonso Cardinal Mistrangelo, Archbishop of Florence. He quickly became the right-hand-man of the chief classicist in the Roman Curia, Nicola Sebastiani, whose official title, Secretary of Briefs to Princes, indicated the original responsibility of his predecessors to compose the official Latin correspondence of the Holy See with the sovereigns of Christendom. Bacci became Sebatsiani's successor upon that scholar's death in 1931. He performed his august duties for the next twenty-nine years until, in 1960, he was given the red hat by John XXIII. After that promotion he served as a member of various curial congregations. In 1964 he published his memoirs, *Con il Latino a Servizio di Quattro Papi*, of which this book is the translation. His views about the changes that swept the Catholic Church in the wake of the Second Vatican Council came to the attention of the public in the last decade of his life and will be noted below. These changes included the free-fall of Latin, which took place at the same time as the equivalent collapse in the groves of academe. For example, in 1964, it was still possible for me, a teenager, to take four years of Latin and read Caesar, Cicero, and Vergil at Lawrence High School, Lawrence, Massachusetts, an immigrant-populated mill town where I received an excellent education in the public school system. Today though, that school, like most American high schools, offers no Latin language instruction whatsoever.

Bacci's great scholarly production was his *Vocabolario Italiano-Latino delle parole moderne e difficili a tradurre* (*Italian-Latin Dictionary of Difficult-to-Translate Modern Words*). This book went through four editions (1944, 1949, 1955, 1963). A companion volume *Inscriptiones, Orationes, Epistulae* (*Inscriptions, Speeches, Letters*) was published at the same time, at first combined with the dictionary in one binding, but subsequently issued as a separate volume. The two together were called *Varia Latinitatis Scripta I and II* (*Assorted Latin Compositions I and II*) and were published in Rome by *Editrice Studium*. After a half-century, Bacci's *Vocabolario* was no longer in print, and the *Libreria Editrice Vaticana* published its two-volume successor, the *Lexicon Recentis Latinitatis* (volume I in 1992, volume II in 1997) under the supervision of one of the cardinal's old assistants, Karl Egger (1914–2003), himself an accomplished lexicographer.

As a churchman, Cardinal Bacci strenuously opposed the direction that the Catholic Church took after the Second Vatican Council. At the time that he published his memoirs (1964), the Council had already issued its constitution *Sacrosanctum Concilium* (1963), which allowed for some use of the vernacular languages in the liturgy, all the while saying that the use of Latin was to be maintained. For this latter reason, Bacci felt able to sign that constitution, which had been carefully drawn up so as to be a consensus document, not in outright contradiction to traditional practice. In the seven years that intervened between the publication of his memoirs and his death, the cardinal witnessed with alarm the attempt, almost entirely and universally successful, to replace Latin in the Church by the modern languages. He made his concern public, and it is of interest briefly to summarize his reasons for doing so.

Bacci was not alone in considering it quite daring, in a system of deductive reasoning such as that of the Catholic Church, to declare that former universal practices and traditions are now all wrong. He feared that the abandonment of Latin would inevitably lead to further changes that would result in the end of the Catholic Church as he knew it. Such a likelihood had been anticipated in times past by competent people:

> The time is coming when Latin will cease to be the language of Catholicism, and with the cessation of Latin, much of the power of Rome will go. (Ignaz von Döllinger in *Alfred Plummer, Conversations with Dr. Döllinger, 1870–1890,* ed. Robrecht Boudens, Leuven: Leuven University Press, 1985, page 15.)

Bacci therefore considered it incorrect to say that the use of the Latin language was of secondary importance and uncorrelated with the survival of the Catholic religion. What is more, the fall of Latin was accompanied by the revision of the Roman Missal, a project against which Bacci, in 1969, issued a famous caution in collaboration with Cardinal Ottaviani. They recognized what is anyway obvious, that when one touches the liturgy in any religion, one gives the impression that everything is up for grabs. Furthermore, to someone like Bacci with a highly developed sensitivity to culture, what he considered the hideous vulgarity of modern liturgical developments was strongly repulsive.

I suspect that Cardinal Bacci would have approved that now, almost fifty years after his death, there has arisen in the Catholic Church a traditional reaction to the changes of the last sixty years, a reaction of sufficient strength to elicit the Apostolic Letter *Summorum Pontificum* of Benedict XVI. This now emeritus pontiff understood that the old ways could not be logically suppressed, nor did he appear to believe that the traditional practices were useless in the maintenance of the Catholic religion.

In such a state of affairs, what is the lesson to be learned from reading Bacci's book today? The reason to study this book is because it presents the arguments for the maintenance of the Latin language in the Roman Catholic Church by the greatest learned authority of our time to speak on the matter. As for myself, I say that the Latin inheritance of Western Europe and of Christendom is a pearl of great value that will never lose its attraction for those who appreciate beauty. It will therefore never be lost absolutely; there will always be some wise men who will preserve it for the edification of future generations. For some of those people the blessings that come from Latin will be the greatest joy of their lives.

This translation was serialized in the newsletters of the Latin Liturgy Association (www.latinliturgy.com) in the period 1989–1990. For the present edition I have corrected a few errors and provided an index.

Anthony Lo Bello
April 29, 2020

INTRODUCTION

In writing these pages, I have kept two goals in mind; the first is to recall, with the necessary reserve and prudence, the relations I have had with four great pontiffs, Pius XI, Pius XII, John XXIII and the reigning Holy Father, Paul VI, popes whom I have had the singular privilege of serving over a long period of time.

These relations and contacts have always aroused in me a profound feeling of admiration and veneration which is sweet to recall, and I hope that those who are now to read these pages will experience the same sentiments.

The second goal is the defense of Latin language and culture in a time when all admit and lament its strong decline. In this frank and calm defense, I have attempted to avoid all exaggeration, every limitation that is restrictive and harmful to the many-faceted and glorious history of this wonderful language, and all sterile, empty, and false erudition which does not teach one to love and enjoy Latin.

In this effort, I have been inspired by the famous Apostolic Constitution *Veterum Sapientia* of John XXIII and the *motu proprio Studia Latinitatis* of the reigning pontiff Paul VI; it is my certain and firm conviction that Latin is not only the official language of the Church, but also the irreplaceable foundation of our culture and civilization.

I

From Florence to Rome

1. LIFE WITH THE SEMINARIANS

In late 1922 I found myself in the post of superior of the archiepiscopal seminary of Florence or, to put it more precisely, of the central seminary, as they used to call it then, because, with the First World War having just ended a few years before, seminarians discharged from military life were converging upon that institution from all the dioceses of Tuscany to complete their final theological studies in that peaceful place and to prepare themselves there suitably for the priesthood.

My job was not easy, quite to the contrary. One had to watch after youngsters, good for sure, but headstrong, who had undergone a crisis more or less severe, and, after having happily overcome it, were with weariness returning to studies and with even greater weariness to the life of recollection and spiritual formation that is recognized as appropriate for priestly formation. Let it suffice to say that they were passing from the barracks to the seminary.

I have always held that the superior of a seminary should never be like a policeman, but rather like a father, or, as I used to tell those dear youngsters, like an older brother, for my own young age at that time did not allow me to adopt a completely paternal attitude. I thought and still do think that exterior discipline is good and even necessary, but that it should be the necessary and spontaneous reflection of an interior discipline that cannot be produced with harsh rebukes and punishments but only induced by understanding, exhortation, and counsel.

I therefore tried to understand those youths as well as I could, to penetrate into the hidden recesses of their souls, and to gain for myself their brotherly confidence; only then did I feel the strength to issue a command, all the while making it understood that my order was directed solely to their welfare.

I recall a very instructive example. In those times, it used to be that every Saturday the seminarians would take turns cleaning and dusting the seminary chapel. Now it so happened that on one Saturday I found myself faced with an absolute refusal on the part of one youngster, who did not want to perform such a menial service. To my repeated requests, he replied, "I came to the seminary to study and pray, not to be the janitor..." I tried in vain to persuade him, assuring him that caring for the cleanliness and decorum of the house of God was not a menial task, but an honor. He remained unconvinced. I then took him by the arm as gently as I could and led him into the chapel; then I said, "You have come to the seminary to study and pray and not to sweep up, as you have told me. Get on your knees here then and pray. Give me the broom, and I'll clean up." And so I did. After having begun that job, I saw out of the corner of my eye that that youth, who was good at heart, was crying instead of praying. Then I saw him get up, come to me, beg my forgiveness, ask for the modest tools needed for the job, and apply himself with the greatest diligence possible to that humble undertaking.

I have recounted this episode in support of a thesis which seems to me to be so right for the proper education of the young clergy, not to eulogize myself, which would anyway be useless. I must even say that on more than one occasion, contrary to my nature, which is not made for unpleasant and vexing decisions, I have had to expel some youngsters from the seminary all of a sudden, because I had the most weighty evidence concerning their conduct and saw that they would be a danger to the others. And even though I always did this with the inspired counsel of my archbishop, I fear that sometimes I was too indulgent and perhaps often too severe. I hope that the Lord will forgive me.

2. THE ORDER TO LEAVE FOR ROME

In 1922, in the fall to be exact, I was at the villa of the central seminary of Florence together with the young seminarians, whom I was teaching dogmatic theology, Latin, and other subjects so that during the summer vacation they might earn the equivalent of an academic year of credit. This villa rises not far from Florence, in the town of Malmantine, on a little hill partly given over to vines and partly covered with tall pines and brown ilices (*lecci*), whence it was called Lecceto. It is an enchanting place, well suited to study and repose. In the lowest part of the hill covered with arbutus, which were showing off their reddish berries in that season, there is a spring of the most clear water, the goal of walks and picnics for the seminarians.

I used to teach outside under a big, leafy ilex, whose thick foliage shaded me and the other young scholars, who formed a circle around me.

At that time Alfonso Cardinal Mistrangelo, Archbishop of Florence, came to Lecceto, either to take a little rest or because, as he used to say, he could feel himself being rejuvenated when he was among the young.

Every day he would take a stroll on the road to Malmantine, and he often took me along for company. I remember how, much to my astonishment, he would, during those walks, recite from memory long excerpts from the comical poem *Malmantine Reconquered*; he was, in fact, not only an outstanding archbishop, but a humanist of tenacious memory and enormous culture.

On that morning, however, he went out accompanied only by his secretary, so that I could give my lesson, but when, on his return, he arrived near the ilex where I was teaching, he stopped and said, "Come to see me at eleven. *Habeo aliquid tibi dicere*; I have something important to tell you." I was a bit worried by those unusual words; I stopped my lesson early, dismissed the young seminarians, and began to walk back and forth in deep thought, mulling over in my mind what on earth it could be that the Cardinal was going to tell me. I first made a brief examination of conscience to figure out if I had done something that deserved to be censured by His Eminence. I didn't think so. Then I thought, "Who knows? Maybe he wants to make me a canon in the cathedral." At that thought I became sad, because I never had the calling to be a canon, and I remembered the saying, "Not knowing what to do with the poor fellow, I made him a canon in the cathedral." Or, maybe he wants to entrust me with a parish? I continued with my soliloquy; being a pastor would not have displeased me, although I would have to leave behind my dear youngsters, to whose formation I was attending with solicitude and affection.

Every once in a while I looked at my watch, and when I saw that it was getting near eleven, I went back to the seminary villa, and, passing by the church, I knelt down in prayer for a few minutes before that beautiful fifteenth-century Madonna above the altar, which appeared at that moment to be watching me with its sweet and maternal gaze.

I then went to the Cardinal's apartment and had myself announced. He received me paternally, as he always did, and invited me to sit down. Then he began, "You know that today, September 30, is the feast of St. Jerome, who was the Latin secretary of Pope Damasus. The people at Rome have asked me for a Latinist, and I thought that you were just the right man to send, so you will go into the Secretariat of State as Latinist; then, later on ... who knows?" At these words I was astounded, and could not express anything but thanks and obedience.

3. MY FIRST MEETING WITH MSGR. MONTINI

About two months later, with the Cardinal's blessing and the affection of my dear seminarians in my heart, I departed anxiously for Rome.

In those days, it took five to six hours to go from Florence to Rome by train; I arrived around noon reeking from the carbon fossil fumes, and for a while I was lodged at the headquarters of the Camaldolese fathers, which at that time was on Via Sistina. I recall that on that very first evening I went out for a little stroll toward the Pincio and met a group of seminarians; I looked at them with nostalgia as if they were my seminarians from Florence, and I cried like a baby.

The next day, accompanied by Msgr. R. Bartolini, himself a Florentine, I reported to the Vatican, to the Secretariat of State. It was a completely new world for me, and I thought I had taken a leap into the dark. However, I found good friends right away, especially

From Florence to Rome

Msgr. Giuseppe Pizzardo, then Substitute of the Secretary of State, who, seeing that I was confused, greeted me with great benevolence and encouraged me, saying right off that I had to dedicate myself entirely to Latin because Msgr. Domenico Spada had just been promoted to be Chancellor of Apostolic Briefs, and they needed a good Latinist.

I immediately set to work with the greatest possible diligence; I wrote in Latin hastily, in every style and on every subject, minute after minute, and I fear that if someone should go to the Archives of the Secretariat of State and track those things down, he would certainly find some mistakes, not only because I had not yet grown accustomed to write in the ancient language of Rome, but also because, as they say, haste makes waste. But Msgr. Pizzardo had all the virtues, as indeed he still has, especially a great delicacy in dealing with people, a great goodness and benevolence toward me. However, he was also always in a hurry, and he showed himself satisfied only when he saw that the job assigned to me was finished.

I spent about a year writing Latin in the Secretariat of State when I saw arrive there a very young priest, far from his home, with an intelligent and penetrating look to him; it was Msgr. Giovanni Battista Montini.

He had just come back from Poland, where he had been for a while secretary at the nunciature, but the cold and damp weather in that country did not agree with his health, which was then delicate and sickly. For this reason, he had been called back to Rome to serve in the Secretariat of State.

We immediately became friends, although, and I say so with all sincerity, whenever I spoke with him, I always felt a sense of awe that prevented me from dealing with him as a colleague, even though he was twelve years my junior and was so open and cordial.

He spoke courteously with whoever approached him; he talked, indeed, but he was not a chatterbox. He worked a lot. As soon as he arrived at the office every morning, he said hello to his friends and sat down to work at his desk, on which there had already been piled up all sorts of things, which Monsignor the Substitute used to deposit daily on his desk, as on the desks of the other *minutanti* as well. (*Minutanti* are priests in the offices of the Secretariat of State who, among other tasks, have the job of preparing the rough drafts of letters to be presented for the superior's signature.)

In this regard, I recall an episode that happened again and again. Certain coworkers, having arrived earlier than Msgr. Montini and seeing on their desks great heaps of papers to be dealt with, took out some of the hardest and clandestinely inserted them into the pile on the desk of Montini. When he arrived, he first sorted out and examined the various papers and could easily see that some of them, on account of their particular content, could not have originally been meant for him; he smiled a little and glanced over at the desk of the colleague who had given him the hardly generous gift, but then began at once, with a seriousness that might appear more like reserve to some but was in fact perfect self-control, to work with the greatest diligence at dispatching all the business.

I also remember that since there was a shortage of Latinists at that time, Msgr. Pizzardo began to entrust various Latin drafts to him, and he would come every once in a while to ask me to look over what he had written. I would timidly suggest some little changes here and there, which he would accept with great humility.

Perhaps for this reason, when, on June 21, 1963, Giovanni Battista Montini was elected Pope, and I, as was the custom, came to his throne in the Sistine Chapel to make my act of obedience and homage, he cordially embraced me and said, "You were my school teacher."

Naturally I blushed at these words of the most profound friendship and thought back to the times when I had the occasion to correct the Latin compositions of the man who had now arrived at the supreme post of Sovereign Pontiff.

I never thought that I was a prophet, nor do I think so now. Nevertheless, during the years when I was working with Msgr. Montini in the Secretariat of State, as I admired his unusual talents, I understood fully that that young priest, so pious, keen, and intelligent, was predestined to play a most important role in the Church.

One day, only a few months after we had begun to work together, I told him all of a sudden, "You, *Monsignore*, will become Substitute of the Secretariat of State." He looked at me in amazement and replied only with a wide sweep of the hand as if to say, "Whatever put that idea in your mind?"

When, however, some years later he was in fact nominated Substitute of the Secretariat of State, he remembered those words of mine, and told me, smiling a bit, "You were a prophet." And I quickly responded, "Very well, and now I'll make another prophecy about you: Your Excellency will one day become Pope." He then shook his head and repeated that wide gesture with his hand.

II

In the Service of Pius XI (1922–1939)

1. MY FIRST EXPERIENCE WITH LATIN IN THE CURIA

As I have said, I arrived in Rome at the Secretariat of State towards the end of 1922, and therefore in the first year of the pontificate of Pius XI; I thus had the opportunity to serve him for about sixteen years.

For sure, during those first years, when I was a *minutante* at the Secretariat of State, my service was indirect in the sense that I was composing the so called cardinalatial letters, that is to say, those that are signed by the Cardinal Secretary of State in the Holy Father's name; many of these were nonetheless quite important.

At that time, the Latin Secretary for Briefs to Princes was Msgr. Nicola Sebastiani, a great genius and concise Latinist in the style of Tacitus, yet ever fluent and elegant.

For those who do not know, the Latin Secretary of Briefs to Princes has that name because he must write up in Latin those letters that the Pope sends to the various heads of state and which he always signs himself. But this is only part of the job, and not the most important part at that. He is also responsible for writing up in Latin the most important Pontifical documents, such as encyclicals, Apostolic Letters, the various texts issued *motu proprio*, Constitutions, and Consistorial Allocutions.

It is, therefore, a position that requires not only great and solid culture, but also poise and prudence in weighing and adjusting thoughts and expressions even to the smallest shades of meaning. These endowments were certainly not lacking in Msgr. Sebastiani.

It happened, however, that in 1928 he was struck down with a grave illness that made him suffer horribly and which, as it progressed, prevented him from working. He had three operations on his mouth, and these three operations deformed his appearance so that he was scarcely recognizable.

For this reason, I had the difficult job of helping him out under the title "Research Assistant". As a matter of fact, from 1929 on, I had to write up all the major pontifical documents myself, though under his guidance and with his advice.

I used to go to the hospital on Corso d'Italia, where he was a patient, and since he had become blind as well, I would write up in Latin documents whose main point I would first give to him in Italian. After finishing a page, I would read it to him to get his opinion, and he would indicate the changes or corrections to be made.

This was certainly a very weighty and difficult procedure for me, not only because of the nature and delicacy of the work itself, but also because that poor *monsignore*, though very virtuous, every once in a while, when things were not going well, would easily become irritated, given the nature of the disease that was tormenting him in an unspeakable manner; he would then lose his temper, but I sympathized with him fully and tried to put up with it as best I could.

In this regard, I recall a very strange episode. In that hospital, there had been assigned to take care of Msgr. Sebastiani a very good nun who was also blessed with plenty of energy, which was necessary in coping with the difficult character of a patient tormented by his grave illness.

One day, while I was working with the poor sick fellow, the aforementioned nun came into the room with dinner. As soon as he saw her, Msgr. Sebastiani shouted (the word is not an exaggeration), "I told you that while I am working with Msgr. Bacci, I do not want to be disturbed!"

The good nun, embarrassed, answered timidly, "But *monsignore*, you need your nourishment. First eat, then work."

"Didn't you understand me? I told you that while I am working I cannot be disturbed. Get out!" repeated Msgr. Sebastiani with the greatest irritation.

But the nun firmly replied with authority, "If you are so intelligent, you should also be a bit more courteous."

At these words, Msgr. Sebastiani replied brusquely, "And how do you know that I am intelligent? How would you know?"

"It doesn't take much to figure it out," she rejoined, at that moment setting the dinner tray down and putting her two hands on her hips as if getting ready to confront someone. She then repeated dryly, "You have a very important position, Latin Secretary of Briefs to Princes. Forgive me for saying so, but you certainly didn't get that job because of your courtesy. I've never seen anyone so discourteous! So, it must have been your intelligence that got you where you are!"

"Oh, all right!" replied Msgr. Sebastiani, "maybe you're right. Give me the tray... Msgr. Bacci will be so kind as to wait while I eat, because we really have to get this work done as soon as possible."

After these words, the sister begged the poor sick man's forgiveness and helped him, with sensitivity and solicitude, to eat his light meal.

2. A BAD MISTAKE IN LATIN

For about three years, life went on like that; Msgr. Sebastiani went back and forth between the hospital and his house, and I followed working tirelessly with him. I must say that for me he was a true teacher and a rough patron. I understood well his horrible physical and moral sufferings, and I tried to show him my complete understanding and gratitude, and he wished me the best, even if he often rebuked me. I am able to say that I owe to him, during three long years of hard work for me and of unspeakable sufferings for him, not only my education in Latin, but also my ability in composing pontifical documents, a thing which is much more difficult than Latin scholarship.

The unrelenting disease that was wearing him out grew worse in the spring of 1931, and in May of the same year, the learned Latinist breathed his last in peace.

With feelings of deep gratitude I composed for him the following long Latin epigraph, in which I recalled, as concisely as possible, his *curriculum vitae* and even his character, harsh by nature, but ever tempered and restrained by his priestly virtue.

NICOLAVS. SEBASTIANI
PATRIA. PONTIANO. ROMANO
INGENIVM. NATVRA. ASPERVM
PAENEQVE. INTRACTABILE
CHRISTIANA. VIRTVTE
COMPESCERE. REGERE. TEMPERARE
SVMMO. NISV. CONTENDIT
THEOLOGICIS. DISCIPLINIS
LATINISQVE
LITTERIS. EXIMIVS
POST. SEDVLO. DATAM. IN
DIOECESI. SVA
ET. IN. LATERANENSI
SACRICOLARVM. EPHEBEO
OPERAM
A. BENEDICTO. XV. P.M. ROMANAE
CVRIAE. ADSCITVS
PRIMVM. A. PONTIFICIIS
DIPLOMATIBVS
DEIN. AB. LITTERIS. LATINIS
POSTREMO. AB. EPISTVLIS
AD. PRINCIPES
NVNCVPATVS
HAEC. SVMMAE. GRAVITATIS. MVNIA
MAGNA. BONORVM. LAVDE
INVIDORVMQVE. OBTRECTATIONE
OBIIT
VNAQVE. SIMVL
IN. SVPREMVM. ADMISSIS
EXPIANDIS. TRIBVNAL
PRAESVL. COOPTATVS
SVAE. ACIE. MENTIS
PRVDENTIQVE. CONSILIO
LABORIS. SOCIOS. ADIVVIT
ATROCI. CANCRI
MORBO. CORRVPTVS
PLVRIESQVE. A. VVLNERARIO

RESECTVS. MEDICO
IMMANITATEM. DOLORIS
INVICTA. ANIMI
FORTITVDINE. TOLERAVIT
OCVLORVM. CAECITAS
QVA. EXTREMIS. LABORAVIT. ANNIS
NON. INERTIS. FVIT. INANISQVE
OTII. CAVSSA
CVM. VIDERETVR. POTIVS
TORNATA. LATINA. ORATIO. EIVS
EX. ORE
NITIDIOR. DEFLVERE
TACITIANA. BREVITATE. POLLENS
AC. SPLENDIDIORIBVS
SENTENTIARVM. LVMINIBVS
CONSPICVA
EODEM. SEMPER. ANIMO
NON. DOLORIBVS. NON
INFIRMITATIBVS. NON
CONTENTIONIBVS. FRACTO
PIISSIME. OBIIT. A. MDCCCCXXXI
ANNOS. NATVS. LXIV

* * *

In grateful memory of Nicholas Sebastiani,
the Supreme Pontiff's Secretary of Briefs
to Princes

Nicholas Sebastiani
born in Ponzano Romano
attempted by constant struggle
to check, restrain, and control
by Christian goodness
a temper that was by nature harsh
and almost intractable.
Famous for his accomplishments

in Theology and Latin,
after working diligently in
his own diocese and
in the Lateran Seminary
he was brought into the Roman Curia
by the Holy Father Benedict xv,
first to compose documents,
then as a Latinist,
and finally as Secretary of Briefs to Princes.
He attended to these most weighty duties
in such a way that
the good praised him well and
the jealous abused him.
At the same time
he was made an official of the
Supreme Tribunal of the
Apostolic Penitentiary
and with his sharp mind
and prudent counsel
was a great help to his colleagues.
Attacked by the horrible disease cancer,
he submitted to several operations
and bore horrible suffering with
an invincibly brave spirit.
In his last years he suffered from blindness,
which did not become for him an excuse
for idle and empty retirement,
but well-turned Latin speech,
shining with the brevity of Tacitus,
bright with the more brilliant lights
of its sentences,
flowed more glitteringly from his mouth.
With the same spirit
unbroken by suffering or
sickness or contentions
he died piously in 1931, 64 years old.

As I recall my predecessor, there comes back to my mind a recollection from long ago. When, thirty-three years ago, after his death, I went to Ponzano Romano, his home town, to take part in the funeral, an exalted prelate, now also dead, uttered the Latin words, "... *animae famuli tui Nicolae* ..."

I shuddered at that great Latin howler *Nicolae*. I remembered the frightening look and deep protests of Msgr. Sebastiani whenever he came across any big blunder in Latin. I immediately had the sensation and fear that the funeral pall would rise up and that the austere figure of the old secretary would get up to shout and protest against the mangling of the language of Rome committed right with his own name.

A few days after the death of Msgr. Sebastiani, I was named his successor as Latin Secretary of Briefs to Princes.

3. "I'VE BEEN WAITING FOR MSGR. BACCI FOR AN HOUR!"

As I said above, I had the great privilege of serving Pius XI during the whole course of his high ministry, almost seventeen years; Papini rightly called him "one of the most complete successors of Peter that Christ ever gave to his Church."

Complete indeed, whether on account of his vast learning, his bravery, his decisive and dynamic character, his clarity of vision that enabled him to see, yea even to foresee, things and quickly draw concrete and practical conclusions from them, or finally his priestly virtue, which he knew how to hide in his straightforward behavior, which was in him the most natural thing in the world.

It has been said that he was given to ordering people about, and that is true, but he knew how to command because before becoming Pope, he had learned how to obey, always to obey the voice of his superiors. Only when one is accustomed to obey can one command equitably and fruitfully.

These facts have been expressed most felicitously by the reigning Pontiff Paul VI in the address given in the auditorium in Rome on June 17, 1964, on the occasion of the 25th anniversary of the death of Pius XI, when he said, "At that time We came to know his mind by direct and happy acquaintance. Everything is true that has been said about his formidable culture, his love for sacred studies, especially those that were historical or bibliographical, of his meditative temperament which led him to go over his recollections, thoughts, and words continually, of his headstrong character, stubborn and hard-working, capable of imperious command, but always tempered by a keen equanimity and often opening up into displays of emotional and moving goodness.... We put his memory forward as worthy of being numbered among those of the best men of our age."

His pontificate was full of great events. It suffices to recall the major one, the Lateran Pacts, which, by resolving a question which had for so many years seemed unsolvable, and by recognizing the full independence of the Pope (who, on account of his supranational office and ministry, cannot be the subject of any state), restored (as Paul VI said) God to Italy and Italy to God. Every disagreement between the Holy See and the Italian government was settled, and the Catholics, previously prevented by the *Non expedit*, were able to enter into the political arena and constitute a powerful bulwark against the forces of dissolution.

Then there was the Year of Jubilee in 1925 and the other extraordinary one in 1933 in memory of the 1900th anniversary of the redemption of the human race by Christ. These were events that inspired a wave of healthy enthusiasm in the whole Catholic world and which brought innumerable bands of praying pilgrims converging on Rome.

But the most important activity, in the spiritual and pastoral sense, was the issuing of his many encyclicals and other pontifical documents; in this I had the fortune to collaborate directly.

Quite rightly did Pius XII utter the following words when he inaugurated the sepulchral monument of this great Pope in St. Peter's Basilica: "One monument alone can worthily represent his spirit, that of his teachings, his examples, his works. Far from decaying with the passing of time, it will appear ever grander and more powerful from generation to generation."

I would not dare to undertake to explain and to comment worthily here on his various encyclicals and other pontifical documents;

In the Service of Pius XI (1922-1939)

that would be an even more difficult job than that which I had as Latin secretary during his long pontificate.

In any case, these documents are there, open to the examination and admiration of all in the official publication of the Holy See, the *Acta Apostolicae Sedis*.

I would only like to recall an episode that occurred while I was fulfilling my sensitive duties, an episode that fully demonstrates this Pontiff's decisiveness and exquisite goodness.

One day, Pius XI summoned me to an audience at a quite unusual hour. I dressed up as usual in the Pian habit and the velvet cape and then went to the pontifical apartment, naturally a bit late and out of breath. Hardly had the Pope seen me when he smiled and said, "Did you really have to pretty yourself up with that fancy habit? It would have been better if you had gotten here five minutes sooner dressed ordinarily." Then he added, "You have to write an encyclical for me as fast as possible. Here are the main points and thoughts which it should set forth," and he gave me a stack of papers, partly handwritten and partly typed. "But make sure," he added firmly and resolutely, "that you prepare this document as soon as possible. It's now the middle of December, and I want to give the printed text to the members of the Sacred College and the prelates of the Curia on the 24th as a sort of Christmas present, when they come to extend their holiday greetings. Can you do it? I want you to do it alone, because I don't like it when one can make out the various styles of different authors, like different threads. Can you do it in time?"

I was by then in a cold sweat, and I answered that I would do everything I could, getting up early in the morning and working late into the night.

"OK," he added, "I am giving you a special blessing to help you and give you strength."

I took leave, kissing his hand, and went straightaway to my apartment to begin to work.

After ten days of hard work, I at last arrived at the end of the project and, after having obtained the first proofs, was able to correct them by pen with the greatest accuracy possible.

I at once applied for an audience and had myself announced without further ado by the *cameriere partecipante* on duty. Hardly had I arrived before His Holiness and knelt down to ask for his blessing when he looked at me in a manner half stern and half smiling and said, "You have been keeping me waiting! But at least you have the proofs with you. Let's take a look."

He read them calmly, stopping every now and then to change some expressions or make some additions. Then he told me, "Bravo! Now have them make the second proofs with the changes I've introduced here, and tonight, I repeat, tonight, at 8 o'clock, come to my private apartment before having it printed in its final form. But be on time, 8 o'clock this evening."

"Certainly, Holy Father," I assured him.

I went back to my study at once, where I made the necessary changes he had pointed out to me. Then I went down to the Vatican Polyglot Press to supervise the second, third, and fourth proofs with the greatest diligence possible. When one is dealing with Latin texts, one has to have at least four proofs, even when, as was then the case, one was working with expert typesetters.

It was getting close to 8 PM, and I was almost ready to go to the Holy Father with the completed and corrected proofs, as he had commanded. However, at the last moment, one page of the proofs, which was still in lead, fell out of the typesetter's hand, so it had to be recomposed, corrected, and recomposed.

It was already 9 PM when I arrived out of breath at the Pope's apartment! I was immediately admitted; I knelt down anxiously, and heard him saying gravely, "I've been waiting for you for an hour! I told you 8 o'clock, and it's already almost 9!"

I started crying as I excused myself and told him about the accident that the typesetter had had. Then Pius XI reverted to his paternal expression and said, "You look pretty tired to me. Take courage; most of the job is done now." He then took the proofs in hand and read them over attentively, dwelling especially on those spots where he had suggested additions or modifications. Then, having finished, he told me half smiling, "Well done. Now you must rest. But have them make at least 500 copies of the encyclical tomorrow because, as

In the Service of Pius XI (1922-1939)

I told you, I want to distribute them on the 24th to the members of the Sacred College and the prelates of the Curia during the audience when they extend their Christmas greetings."

I thanked him, and with my face still soaked with sweat and tears, let myself out with a great sigh of relief.

On the following day, a *cameriere partecipante* came to visit me in my apartment, and as he gave me a very long package, which looked like the architrave of a door, he said to me, "The Holy Father sends you this present. It's just right for you, and he ordered me to tell you to use it because you need it."

I begged the kind messenger to please express to the Holy Father my devoted and humble thanks.

4. A MONUMENT TO GARIBALDI AND ONE IN COMMEMORATION OF VATICAN I

Many perhaps do not realize that Pius IX, on the occasion of the celebration of the First Vatican Ecumenical Council, had planned to have a great marble and bronze monument constructed and placed on the summit of the Janiculum Hill; it was the work of various artists and consisted of a huge base, on whose sides were represented, in marble bas-relief, on the left the solemn inauguration of the great assembly with the Pope himself sitting on his throne surrounded by the Council Fathers and, on the right, two angels who were holding up the triple crown and the keys, symbol of the supreme authority of the Pontiff. Upon this base there was supposed to rise up a high column surmounted by a plinth, on whose sides were sculpted five monsters symbolizing the main heresies, and higher up there was erected the bronze statue of St. Peter, who in one hand held the keys, the sign of his power over the whole Church, and with his other hand was giving a blessing.

Everything was almost ready to be set up on the Janiculum Hill, but then Rome was taken and the Ecumenical Council suspended, and the various parts of the monument had to be placed in the *Cortile della Pigna*, in the Vatican, where they remained until 1936. By order of Leo XIII, two marble plaques with the following inscriptions had been set into the wall above them as a memorial.

I.

PIVS. IX. PONTIFEX. MAXIMVS
CONCILII. OECVMENICI. VATICANI
AB. SE INDICTI. INCHOATI
MONVMENTVM
IN. IANICVLI. VERTICE
STATVENDVM. DECREVIT
ANNO. CHR. MDCCCLXXI

II.

LEO. XIII. PONTIFEX. MAXIMVS
INIVRIA. TEMPORVM. PROHIBITVS
TVTIORE. IN. LOCO
INTRA. VATICANI. SEPTA
ERIGI. IVSSIT
ANNO. CHR. MDCCCLXXXV

* * *

I.

Pius IX Supreme Pontiff
ordered that this monument
of the Ecumenical Council of the Vatican
convened and begun by him
be set up on the top of the Janiculum Hill
in the year of Christ 1871.

II.

Leo XIII Supreme Pontiff
on account of the bad times
ordered it to be placed in a safer location
within the walls of the Vatican
in the year of Christ 1885.

On Pentecost Sunday, 1936, I was summoned by the Holy Father at an unusual hour; I went at once to the audience, not only with the accustomed haste, but also with a certain anxiety because, on

In the Service of Pius XI (1922-1939)

account of the unusual summons, I supposed that His Holiness was going to entrust me with the composition of some encyclical or other important and urgent Pontifical document. However, when I arrived, Pius XI, seeing that I was a bit out of breath and troubled, looked at me with a smile, and said jokingly (which was something quite unusual for him):

> Don't be afraid: *noli timere*. We are entrusting you with a very easy and even enjoyable task. Maybe you know (I didn't) that Our predecessor Pius IX had planned to erect a great monument which was to be set up on the Janiculum Hill in memory of the Ecumenical Council of the Vatican. But then came the war, the fall of Rome, and the interruption of the Council, and on the Janiculum there went up instead the statue of Garibaldi. Now We, who made the Lateran treaty, do not want to discomfit Garibaldi. Times have changed. But We would like a worthy place for that poor monument, which sits there in the courtyard as if it had been thrown into prison. We have therefore considered putting it in the Vatican Gardens, on that little eminence that divides the two branches of the old Leonine Walls and which is called "The Observatory". We consequently entrust to you the task of composing five Latin epigraphs, which We would like to have sculpted into the plinth that supports the statue of St. Peter, precisely on the five sides that have the monsters that represent the heresies. We would like to replace the monsters, which are not even artistically admirable, with your inscriptions, which We predict will be more beautiful.

Having said that, he dismissed me, wishing me a Happy Pentecost.

I naturally fulfilled the Holy Father's order in the best way I could, and the five inscriptions were approved and sculpted in the places indicated. Here they are:

I.
VATICANI. CONCILII. MONVMENTVM
QVOD. PIVS. IX. IN. IANICVLI. VERTICE. ERIGENDVM
DECREVERAT. QVODQVE
LEO. XIII
INTRA. VATICANI. SAEPTA. STATVERAT
PIVS. XI. PONTIFEX. MAXIMVS
HEIC. COLLOCANDVM. CVRAVIT
ANNO. MDCCCXXXVI

II.
QVAE
SACRA. VATICANA. SYNODVS
DE. VERA. FIDE
VNOQVE. ECCLESIAE. REGIMINE
SANXIT. POPVLOS. OMNES
IN. VNVM. CONGREGATOS. OVILE
AD. APOSTOLICAE. PETRAE. VNITATEM
FELICITER. REDVCANT

III.
IMPETRET. A. DEO
APOSTOLORUM. PRINCEPS
CHRISTIANORVM. VT. NOMEN
FLOREAT. VIGEAT. PROPAGETVR
VTQVE. ERRORES. VERITATI
VITIA. VIRTVTI. CONCEDANT

IV.
QVI
AD. INTERITVM. VSQVE. HVMANI
AEVI. IN. SVCCESSORIBVS. SVIS
VIVIT. DOCET. REGIT
IPSE. OPITVLANTE. NVMINE
EX. HAC. CATHOLICAE. VERITATIS
ARCE. QVOSLIBET. HOSTILES
PROHIBEAT. INCVRSVS

V.
QVI
HAC. IN. AMOENITATE. LOCI
CIRCVM. DEHISCVNT. REDOLENTQVE. FLORES
ILLIVS. VIRTVTVM. DECORIS
QVO. CATHOLICVM. RENIDEAT
NOMEN
IMAGINES. PERPETVO. SVNTO

* * *

I.

Pius XI Supreme Pontiff
ordered that there be erected on this spot
the monument of the Vatican Council
that Pius IX had commanded to be set up
on the Janiculum Hill
and which Leo XIII had placed
inside the Vatican Walls.

II.

May what
the sacred Vatican Council decreed
concerning the true faith and the Papal
government of the Church
happily bring all nations back to the
one flock
and to the unity of the Apostolic See.

III.

May the Prince of the Apostles
obtain from God the favor
that the Christian name
flourish, thrive and spread
and that errors yield to truth,
and defects to perfection.

IV.

May he who lives, teaches, and reigns
through his successors to the end of time
with the help of God
throw back all hostile assaults from this
fortress of Catholic truth.

V.

May the fragrant flowers
that bloom in this beautiful spot
forever symbolize those glorious virtues
that the name *Catholic* calls to mind.

Whoever visits the Vatican Gardens can read these short Latin epigraphs even today. The upper part of the commemorative monument, which was to rise on the Janiculum on the spot where the statue of Garibaldi stands today, was erected, by order of Pius XI, on the indicated spot, that is, on the little hill called "The Observatory"; the great column was put to other uses. The two Latin inscriptions of Pius IX and Leo XIII were immured hard by on the inside of the Leonine Walls. Four grand, graceful marble angels now lie near the hedge of box trees that surrounds the monument, and with their wings downward and their eyes toward heaven, they seem to smile serenely as they contemplate the latest developments in this matter. Some other ornamental fragments can be found here and there in the gardens, and the two great bas-reliefs, which were to be incorporated into the lower base of the monument, have been set into the outer walls of the quaint little house that was once the headquarters of the superintendent of the gardens and is today the seat of the superintendent of Vatican excavations. It is interesting to see how one of these, the one with the pontifical triple crown held up by two angels, carries down below the coats of arms of two Popes, Pius IX and Leo XIII, a fact which clearly indicates that some parts of this historic monument were only finished in the pontificate of the latter.

When I climb back up the Vatican Hill, as I do almost every evening, I look thoughtfully on those fragments of a great historical monument,

In the Service of Pius XI (1922-1939) 25

especially at the bronze statue of the first Pope, St. Peter, who, from the spot of his martyrdom, turns toward the Vatican Basilica where the Second Vatican Council is being celebrated, and blesses with his right hand as if to guarantee for it a fruitful and salutary outcome.

The course of human affairs passes and changes continually, but the Church remains, and the beneficent light of Rome shines even today on the whole world, as it did yesterday, and as it will tomorrow.

5. PIUS XI AT THE END

Pius XI had a very strong constitution. When he was young, he used to climb the Alps; then he became a librarian. First he learned how to climb mountains in order to enjoy from those solitary heights the panorama below and to feel as if from a little closer the height of heaven and the presence of God; later, having become a librarian, he made other ascents, those of human thought and of the different civilizations through the exhausting course of the centuries. These two occupations, Alpinist and librarian, strengthened his body and at the same time his mind, making familiar to him, through constant study, quite a breadth of human knowledge.

He had a will of steel and a tireless capacity for work; he could say of himself, even when he faced the gravest difficulties, *"Frangar, non flectar!"* I will break, but I will not bend!

For this reason, everyone was not only saddened but also surprised when, in the beginning of 1936, the word spread that the Pope was sick, that he was tired, that he had to take a necessary period of repose. Such was what the doctors ordered, but his will could not bear inactivity, even that of a well-earned rest. "The Pope," he used to say, "must either work or die. That is his inexorable duty!"

All the same, at the insistence of the doctors and of his most intimate associates, he had not really to rest but to relent a bit from his excessive work and to submit himself to the necessary treatments.

After a certain lapse of time, his strength unexpectedly returned, a return which he attributed to the intercession of St. Theresa of the Child Jesus, whom he used to call the star of his pontificate. (St. Theresa of the Child Jesus was beatified by Pius XI in 1923 and canonized by him in 1925.)

This miraculous return of strength gave him the opportunity to return to work as before and even more than before.

I remember one day when I was summoned to an audience in his private apartment on account of a job that he wanted to entrust to me. Because of his sickness, many months had passed without my having received such an invitation. When I saw him sitting in a long reclining chair, he gave me the impression of a healthy man who had overcome a long illness. For this reason, after I had kissed his hand, the following words came spontaneously to my lips, "Holy Father, I see with great pleasure that Your Holiness has entirely recovered."

He asked me to sit down, and then with a light smile he said, "St. Theresa of the Child Jesus is the one who has obtained for me this grace of being able once more to work for a little while."

"For a long while," I interrupted gently, "Your Holiness surely knows how Leo XIII almost reached his ninety-fourth year, and Your Holiness has a much stronger constitution than he had."

"Let's not make useless compliments," the Pope said, weighing each word and becoming a bit solemn. Then, recovering his serenity, he added in a playful manner, "Few live into their nineties, and do you know why?"

I was a bit confused and did not know how to answer. But the Pope continued, still joking, "What? Don't you know why few live to be ninety?... It doesn't take much to figure it out... Because they die first!"

I, who was not used to enjoying the confidence and even less the jokes of Pius XI, remained silent still. And it was he who broke the silence by handing me some papers which I was to use in preparing a Latin document as soon as possible.

After about two years, alas, the Pope's state of health got worse again, and this aroused the gravest concern.

The year 1939 was a particularly solemn year because of the coincidence of the sixtieth anniversary of his priesthood, the twentieth of his episcopacy, and the tenth of the Conciliation and the Lateran Pacts. Pius XI wanted to solemnize the triple anniversary in the most worthy and fruitful manner possible.

In the Service of Pius XI (1922-1939)

He had decided to invite the Italian bishops to solemnize, on February 11, the event that is held to be the most important of his pontificate, the Conciliation. To this end, he began to prepare an allocution that was to be delivered on that day to the assembled bishops.

Everyone knows that after the happy conclusion of the Lateran Pacts, the waters were troubled between the Italian government and the Holy See. Benito Mussolini, a few days after February 11, 1929, pronounced an address that caused much sorrow and disquiet to the Pope and Christianity. Then followed the measures taken against Catholic Action, then the alliance with Adolf Hitler and consequently the famous encyclicals of Pius XI in which he condemned the errors of fascism and racism (*Non Abbiamo Bisogno*, June 29, 1931; *Mit Brennender Sorge*, March 14, 1937).

All, therefore, were awaiting the coming Papal allocution to the Italian episcopate with a certain anxiety and preoccupation. The Holy Father, in spite of his condition of health, which was getting worse day by day, composed his address with an indefatigable zeal. To the doctors and to his most intimate familiars, who were gently exhorting him not to tire himself too much and to put off his talk to another more opportune time, he replied that the address was necessary; the bishops were already beginning to arrive in Rome, and the thing could therefore not be put off any longer.

"If I shall not be able to go down into the Vatican Basilica, I shall have myself carried in the *Sedia Gestatoria* to the Hall of Benedictions, and if I cannot even make it there, I shall convene the bishops here in my private apartment. And if I cannot even talk, I shall have someone else read what I have to say." He was immovable: *Frangar, non flectar!*

Through this supreme effort of will power, he was able to finish writing and revising his speech. It was February 9, and the allocution was scheduled for the morning of the 11th. But the state of his health got so worse that in the opinion of his doctors, the end now seemed near.

As it turned out, Pius XI peacefully breathed his last on February 10 at 5:31 AM. The Italian bishops, who were gathered in Rome to hear his last allocution, were instead able to attend with emotion his solemn funeral. (Parts of his allocution were inserted into a letter that Pope John XXIII addressed to the Italian episcopate on February 6, 1959;

see *L'Osservatore Romano* of February 9, 1959.) One could say that he died in the trenches, the heroic trenches of his own duty.

As Secretary of Briefs to Princes, I had the sad duty to compose his funeral oration which, inscribed on parchment and read by me before the Sacred College on the last day of the *novendiali*, was then deposited with the body in the sepulchral niche.

I hope that I do nothing that my readers will not appreciate when I repeat here the eulogy together with the four Latin inscriptions that I wrote and that were set up on the four sides of the *castrum doloris*, or catafalque.

Quattuor, qui sequuntur, tituli honorario tumulo inscripti cernebantur, cum in Vaticana Basilica, coram Sacro Patrum Cardinalium Collegio ingentique multitudine, justa funebria Pio XI Pont. Max. celebrata fuere a. MDCCCCXXXIX.

I.

INTEGERRIMVS. VERITATIS. CVSTOS
ERVMPENTES. ERRORES
INVICTO. PECTORE. REPRESSIT
PROFLIGAVIT
ABERRANTES. REVOCANS. OMNES
AD. CATHOLICAE. FIDEI. VNITATEM

II.

CVLTORIS. HVMANITATIS. FAVTOR
SACRAS. PROFANASQVE. DISCIPLINAS
PROVEXIT
STVDIORVM. DOMICILIA
EXCITAVIT
AD. MELIOREM. FORMAM. REDEGIT

III.

VNIVERSAE. HOMINVM. FAMILIAE
TOT. DISCIDIIS. DOLORIBVSQVE
ANXIAE

FRATERNAM. CONCORDIAM
IVSTITIA. DVCE. CARITATE. AVSPICE
PATERNO. SVASIT. ANIMO

IV.
ACERRIMVS. IVSTAE. LIBERTATIS
VINDEX
INIVRIAS. QVASLIBET. ECCLESIAE
ILLATAS. COMPESCVIT
VETERRIMAQVE. DISSENSIONIS
CAVSSA. DELETA
PACEM. ITALIAE
INTEGRIS. RELLIGIONIS. IVRIBVS
RESTITVIT

* * *

The four inscriptions that follow were inscribed on the catafalque when the customary funeral rites of the Supreme Pontiff Pius XI were celebrated in 1939 in the Vatican Basilica before the Sacred College of Cardinals and an enormous multitude.

I.
The most upright guardian of the truth
with invincible courage repressed and beat back
all errors as they burst forth
recalling all those who err
to the unity of the Catholic faith.

II.
Patron of scholars
he promoted both sacred and profane
studies.
He erected schools
and improved those already standing.

III.

In his paternal spirit
he recommended brotherly harmony
under the rule of justice and the sway of love
to the whole human family disturbed by so
many divisions and sorrows.

IV.

The most uncompromising defender of justice and
liberty,
he kept to a minimum whatever damages
were inflicted on the Church,
and maintaining whole the rights of religion,
he restored peace with Italy
removing the long-standing cause
for dissension.

Ellogium Pii xi Pont. Max. quod, arte exima in assimulata membrana inscriptum, coram Sacro Patrum Cardinalium Collegio ingentique multitudine, Antonius Bacci ab Epist. ad Principes in Vaticanae Basilicae majestate recitavit, ac postea fuit in eiusdem Pontificis tumulum inclusum.

PIUS XI PONT. MAX.

Ambrosius Achilles Damianus Ratti Deusii, in oppido Mediolanensis Archidioecesis, die xxxi mensis Maji, anno a rep. sal. mdccclvii natus, insequenti die lustrali Sacri fontis aqua expiatus est.

Prima juventute ineunte, ad sacerdotium divino instinctu vocatus, cum ad Divi Petri Martyris, tum Modiciae, Mediolani, Romae in sacras profansque disciplinas summa cum laude incubuit; atque die xx Decembris, anno mdccclxxix, in Lateranensi Archibasilica sacerdotalem ordinem dignitatemque pientissimo suscepit animo.

Primum in patrio Seminario sacrorum alumnis instituendis sollertem dedit operam; deinde vero, pro eximiis, quibus pollebat, litterarum optimarumque artium ornamentis, Ambrosianae ac

In the Service of Pius XI (1922-1939)

mox Vaticanae Bibliothecae Praefectus renuntiatus est; quo in munere obeundo, sive eruditis hominibus consilio assidens, sive operosas peragens ipsemet investigationes, de humanis divinisque disciplinas optime meruit.

At ad latiorem laboris honorisque campum Dei nutu vocabatur; siquidem saeviente fere ubique per Europam immani bello, in Poloniam sequester pacis mittitur: ibique mandato Summi Pontificis Benedicti xv, qua Visitator Apostolicus, qua Nuntius, non modo Jesu Christi Vicarii partes actuosa sustinuit navitate, sed illud etiam "antemurale christianitatis", novo oborto infensissimo bello, strenuo vigore ac singulari ausu tuitus est.

Rebus tandem compositis, anno MDCCCCXXI in patriam reversus, Mediolanensi Ecclesiae Pontifex praeficitur, ac Romanae purpurae majestate, summo cum omnium plausu, decoratur.

Perbrevi solummodo temporis spatio Ambrosiana urbs potuit tanto Pastore perfrui; etenim, Benedicto xv, in maximo catholici orbis maerore, e vivis sublato, in ejus locum, die vi mensis Februari anno MDCCCCXXII, gratulantibus christianis omnibus, suffectus est, sibique Pio xi nomen indidit.

Innumerabilia sunt ac miranda prorsus quae in Dei gloriam et Catholicae Ecclesiae incrementum per septem et decem annos in Summo Pontificatu gessit. Sacras expeditiones—missis usquequaque gentium Evangelii praeconibus, pluribusque conditis Dioecesibus— summopere propagavit, provexit; sacrorum alumnos—novis excitatis Seminariis, Athenaeis studiorumque Universitatibus, ac sapientibus editis normis—ad litterarum altiorumque disciplinarum studia cohortatus est; insurgentes errores atque haereses, praeclarissimis impertitis documentis, damnavit, compescuit; itemque, ut cleri operam faciliorem latioremque efficeret, in sacri Apostolatus partes eos omnes cooptavit, qui, in Catholicae Actionis agminibus militantes, Jesu Christi Regnum omni ope tutantur, augent, promovent.

Publicas cum Civitatibus necessituidines quam impensissime fovit; ac novas cum Rebuspublicis non paucis conventiones sanxit: in quibus illae notatu dignae, quae inter Apostolicam Sedem et Italae Regnum felicissime initae sunt.

Ter Jubilaea sacra catholico orbi indixit; quinto scilicet hujus saeculi exeunte lustro; quinquagesimo dein sacerdotii sui vertente anno; decimo nono denique revoluto saeculo a peracta humani generis Redemptione.

Plurimis evangelicae virtutis heroibus vel Beatorum, vel Sanctorum Caelitum honores decrevit; eosdemque christiano populo universe ad imitandos proposuit.

Quapropter tot curis laboribusque fractus, die x mensis februarii, anno MDCCCCXXXIX, complorantibus cujusvis ordinis hominibus ac gentibus, in Christo placidissime quievit.

Animo fuit invicto, ingenio acri, voluntate tenacissima.

Veritatem omnibus, etsi non gratam, aperie profitebatur.

Sacrosancta Ecclesiae jura adversus conatus quoslibet, per omnem Pontificatus sui decursum, toto pectore adseruit, vindicavit.

Vixit annos LXXXI, menses VIII, dies X; in Summo Pontificatu annos XVII, dies IV.

Sanctissime Pater, perpetuo vivas in Christo, ac sempiterna beatitate fruare.

* * *

Here is the funeral oration for the Supreme Pontiff Pius XI, inscribed with great art on parchment and recited in the majesty of the Vatican Basilica before the Sacred College of Cardinals and an immense multitude by Antonio Bacci, the Secretary for Briefs to Princes, and afterwards enclosed in the tomb of the same Pontiff.

PIUS XI. SUPREME PONTIFF

Ambrogio Achille Damiano Ratti was born at Desio, in the archdiocese of Milan, on May 31, 1857 and was reborn through sacred baptism on the next day.

From his earliest youth he felt inspired from on high to follow the way of the priesthood, and he received his education first at the College of St. Peter Martyr, at that time in Monza, then at the Milanese seminary, and finally at Rome, where he completed his studies with the highest grades in both sacred and profane subjects.

In the Service of Pius XI (1922-1939)

On December 20, 1879, he received the priestly ordination and dignity in the Lateran Archbasilica with great edification and piety. He was summoned to be a professor on the faculty of his native seminary, where he did diligent and highly appreciated work in the education and instruction of the young clergy of that archdiocese; after that, on account of his distinguished gifts of brilliance and culture, he was nominated Prefect of the Ambrosian Library and then of the Vatican Library, in which offices he was of great service to students and earned the highest merit by his published works on important topics.

But soon Divine Providence called him to an even larger field of work, for when the First World War was raging throughout almost all of Europe, he was, because of the confidence that the Supreme Pontiff Benedict xv had in him, sent off as a messenger of peace, first as Apostolic Visitor and then as Nuncio in Poland, where, in the name of His Holiness, he carried on an untiring activity, defending with his robust strength and zeal that "outpost of Christianity" in the grave perils of yet another war.

And finally, after an intense and happy work of conciliation, he was called back home and made Archbishop of Milan and distinguished with the sacred purple of the cardinalate.

But the Ambrosian archdiocese was only able to enjoy the strong and secure leadership of this great pastor for a brief time, for when Benedict xv, to the immense grief of all, departed this life, he was called to succeed him on February 6, 1922 to the applause and joy of all Christendom, and took the name of Pius xi.

Innumerable and marvelous were the initiatives and works that he undertook during the seventeen years of his pontificate for the glory of God and the increase of the Catholic Church. He promoted the Catholic missions with a tireless zeal, sending out the heralds of the Gospel to the extremities of the universe and creating new dioceses there. He exhorted those destined for the sanctuary energetically to pursue both sacred and profane studies by founding new seminaries, new Atheneums, new universities, which he took care to have regulated by wise norms. He condemned severely in his wise writings every heresy and error against faith and morals, and when he saw that the apostolate of the clergy needed assistance to cope with ever growing needs, he called in the laity, uniting them under the banner of Catholic Action, so that they could give their active collaboration in defending, increasing, and efficaciously promoting the Kingdom of Jesus Christ on earth.

He favored diplomatic relations between the Holy See and the nations and sanctioned not a few new concordats with several states; among these concordats the famous one is that which was happily concluded between the Holy See and the Kingdom of Italy.

He three times declared a Holy Year of Jubilee for the whole Catholic world, firstly in 1925, secondly on the fiftieth anniversary of his ordination, and thirdly after nineteen centuries had passed since the moment of human redemption.

He raised many heroes of Christian virtue to the honors of the altar with the title of Blessed or Saint, setting them up before the clergy and people as examples and intercessors.

Exhausted by such intense cares and tireless activity, on February 10, 1939, to the grief of all, he peacefully breathed his last with the name of Jesus on his lips.

He was of unconquerable spirit, of lively and quick genius, of the most tenacious will.

He always dared to tell the truth openly to everyone, even when it was not welcome.

Throughout the whole of his pontificate with brave heart he proclaimed and defended against every attempt at usurpation all the sacrosanct rights of the Church.

He lived 81 years, 8 months, and 10 days.

His pontificate lasted 17 years and 4 days.

Most Holy Father, may you live forever in Christ in the enjoyment of the sempiternal happiness of heaven.

III
In the Service of Pius XII (1939-1958)

1. THE BEST PREPARED THROUGH WISDOM AND DIVINE GRACE

The conclave of 1939 took place at a moment of great apprehension, and I would say almost of anxiety. As I pointed out in the preceding chapter, relations between the Italian government and the Holy See, after the joy and exultation of the Conciliation, had become troubled. What is more, Mussolini had made a pact with Hitler, the famous Rome-Berlin Axis. The horizon was becoming darker and darker, and people were already beginning to talk of war, that long and horrible Second World War, which in fact broke out only a few months later.

One of the duties of my office was to compose the so-called *Oratio de Eligendo Pontifice*, a Latin address that the Secretary of Briefs to Princes must customarily give before the Sacred College at the beginning of the conclave.

The famous American author Henry Morton Robinson, in his fanciful style, describes those anxious days as follows (and not always accurately), quoting at length from my Latin oration in his novel, *The Cardinal*:

> On the morning of that day [March 1, 1939], sixty-two cardinal electors attended a Missa Solemnis sung by Cardinal Pignatelli di Belmonte in the Pauline Chapel, the "parish church" of the Vatican. Attentively they listened to an eloquent sermon delivered in Latin by Monsignor Antonio Bacci, Undersecretary of Letters to Foreign Rulers. Begging the sufferance of his listeners, Monsignor

Bacci stressed the solemnity of the occasion, the mournful state of the world, and the fearful responsibility that rested upon the electors of a new Pope. He exhorted his hearers to bear in mind that the man they were about to choose as the Keeper of the Pontifical Keys must be the ablest, most saintly among their number.

"You must ask yourselves, Most Eminent Lords," said the speaker, "which among you has the character to resist the new paganism of State that is even now preparing to engulf the world with blood and force. You must search your hearts to discover which of your noble fellowship is best fitted by wisdom and divine grace to defend the Church, and, indeed, civilization itself, against the dangers that await us or, rather, my Lords, at this very moment surround us. Let me use the metaphor of the navigator; the man elected by you will be called upon to pilot St. Peter's bark through seas infested by ice floes that even now are breaking loose from the fearful glacier of barbarism."

Ornate? Perhaps. Yet when the orator rounded into his peroration, Stephen thought that Monsignor Bacci's sermon was as fine a combination of form and substance as he had ever heard.

The novelist continues by describing as minutely as possible, as if he had himself been present, all the things that took place during the conclave at the various meetings and scrutinies; he then concludes with these words:

At five-thirty that afternoon a plume of white smoke rising over the roof of the Sistine Chapel told the multitude in St. Peter's Square that a new Pope had been elected.

The bells of Rome's four hundred churches, led by *il campanone,* the eleven-ton master of St. Peter's, were tolling the Angelus when Cardinal Caccia Dominioni appeared in the central balcony overlooking the piazza.

Loudspeakers carried the traditional announcement in Latin: "I announce to you a great joy. We have a Pope. He is my most eminent and reverend lord Eugenio..."

A tremendous shout arose from half-a-million throats. Everyone knew who Eugenio was. Cries of "Viva il Papa" drowned out the pealing bells. But the real ovation occurred when the Pope himself appeared on the central balcony of St. Peter's to give his blessing *Urbi et Orbi*. When the thunderous tumult had spent itself, all knelt in silence while the Pope blessed the city and the world.

Watching the pontiff's hand lifted in benediction, Stephen understood the serene truth of the Italian proverb, "The Pope dies; the Pope lives." Two hundred and sixty-one wearers of the triple tiara had faded from the earthly scene, but the papacy itself—now embodied in the lean and fearless person of Eugenio Pacelli—was deathless and eternal.

At that solemn moment, I was in St. Peter's Square with the jubilant multitude. I must confess that even I was overcome with profound emotion, and the tears were streaming from my eyes. It was a page from history that one cannot forget.

Two hours later, the new Pope summoned me. I anxiously entered his private apartment and found him still looking overcome and, I would say, a bit crushed by it all; the weight of the pontificate was overwhelming his slender figure. Only his lively and penetrating eyes were the same as I remembered from years past.

He invited me to stay with him late into the night so that I could write up in Latin, under his personal direction, the address that he had to make to the whole world on the morning following.

2. THE WAR

The political situation in Europe was getting worse day by day; dark storm clouds were appearing on the horizon. The word *war* was on everyone's lips.

Pius XII called more and more for peace and harmony, but the world seemed to be on the brink of an abyss.

On August 24, 1939, when the imminent danger of the next world war was just around the corner, His Holiness addressed the following radio message to the world's leaders and peoples, a father's cry of courage and incomparable love:

> A grave hour has once again struck for the great human family; an hour of awful deliberations from which neither Our heart nor Our spiritual authority can distance themselves, for God has given them to Us to lead souls on the path of justice and peace.
>
> We stand with all of you who bear the weight of so great a responsibility at this moment, so that through Our voice, you may hear the voice of that Christ from whom the world learned the lessons of life, and in whom millions upon millions of souls place their faith during an emergency in which his word alone can prevail over all the uproar on earth.
>
> We stand with you, leaders of nations, politicians and soldiers, writers, men of the radio, orators, and as many others as have influence over the thought and actions of their fellow men and responsibility for their fate.
>
> We, armed with nothing other than the word of truth, far above public contests and passions, speak to you in the name of God, after whom every family in heaven and on earth is named, of Jesus Christ, our Lord, who wanted all men to be brothers, of the Holy Ghost, gift of God Most High, the inexhaustible fountain of love in our hearts.
>
> Today, when, despite Our repeated appeals and Our particular concern, fears of a bloody world war are ever more stirred up, today, when emotions are raised to such

a pitch that it seems likely that the horrible machinery of war will soon be set loose, We, as a father, make a new and more fervid appeal to world leaders and peoples, to the former, that, setting aside accusations, threats, and grounds for mutual distrust, they try to solve their present differences by the one proper way, by common, binding agreements, and to the latter, that, in calmness and serenity, without unseemly demonstrations, they encourage the peaceful initiatives of their leaders.

It is through the force of reason, not that of arms, that justice makes progress. Empires not founded upon justice are not blessed by God. Politics free of morality betrays the very ones who practice it.

The danger is near, but there is still time.

Nothing is lost by peace; everything can be lost through war. Let men go back to understanding one another. Let them go back to negotiating. By negotiating in good will and with respect for each other's rights, they will perceive that an honorable outcome is never impossible when one has sincere and factual discussions.

They will become great with true greatness if, by imposing silence on the voices of passion, both public and private, and by giving reason full rein, they will have spared their brothers their blood, and their fatherland its ruin.

May the Almighty grant that the voice of this father of the Christian family, of this servant of the servants of God, who bears, unworthily to be sure, but nonetheless really the person, word, and authority of Jesus Christ, may find a willing and immediate acceptance in the hearts and minds of men.

Let the brave hear Us, that they may not become weak through injustice. Let the powerful hear Us, if they want their power to work not the destruction of peoples, but their prosperity, protection, and tranquility in their station and work.

We beg them through the blood of Christ, whose strength, which conquered the world, was meekness in life and death. And as We beg them, We know and feel that We have with Us all those who are upright of heart, all those who hunger and thirst for justice, all those who are already suffering every pain through the evils that life brings. We have with Us the hearts of the mothers, that beat with Ours, the fathers, who would have to abandon their families, the lowly, who toil and do not understand, the innocent, on whom the frightening threat weighs down, the young, gallant knights with the purest and noblest ideals. And with Us is the soul of this old Europe, the work of Christian faith and genius. With Us is all humanity, which waits for justice, bread, and liberty, not iron, which kills and destroys. With Us is that Christ, who made brotherly love his fundamental and solemn commandment, the substance of his religion, and the promise of salvation for men and nations.

Mindful, at last, that human activities have no value without divine help, We invite everyone to turn his gaze on high and ask the Lord with fervid prayers to send down his abundant grace on this tortured world, to appease men's angers, to reconcile their souls, and to make shine the dawn of a more serene future. In this expectation, and with this hope, We impart to all from Our heart Our paternal benediction.

If those in authority had listened to this fatherly cry of alarm, the human race would have been spared years of horrible suffering and fratricidal slaughter. But a sort of intoxication with power and domination had taken over the minds of the two dictators, and the war was unleashed first on Europe, and then upon the whole world.

Once Pius XII saw that there was no way of avoiding the war, he devoted himself entirely to mitigating its horrible effects and to trying to bring about by every means possible that the great conflict finally end in a just arrangement.

In the Service of Pius XII (1939-1958)

All know his charitable initiatives, his many calls to fraternal concord, his radio messages of encouragement and peace.

All know that the small Vatican City State and its extraterritorial properties had become places of sanctuary for many whose very lives were threatened. They were all taken in, without discrimination as to religion or race.

All know that one day, while the incendiary bombs were reducing the populous San Lorenzo quarter of Rome to a heap of ruins, his white figure, together with that of the reigning Pontiff, then Msgr. Montini, appeared unexpectedly amidst the wreckage and the terror of the citizens, who by then had found in him alone a refuge and a consoler. His white cassock was stained with the blood of the poor wounded.

A pontiff, who was by nature meek, had found the strength and the courage of Leo the Great. And at the end of the war, when the final catastrophe seemed to be closing in on the city, he, by his word alone, which at that supreme moment had become almost formidable, knew how to avoid the scourge in a way that appeared miraculous. For this, with good reason, the people acclaimed him as the *Defensor Civitatis*, the Defender of the City. The people, when they are not instigated, never err; *Vox populi, vox Dei*, the voice of the people is the voice of God.

For this reason, they are in manifest error who now accuse Pius XII of weakness and acquiescence on account of his policy with regard to the war and the war crimes. Nothing is more false: it was never a case of *weakness*, but of *prudence*. He condemned the war and the exterminations frequently, but in a way so as to save what could be saved and not to make things even worse.

He often told me, when I submitted my rough drafts of certain kinds of documents, "You must avoid certain harsh expressions. I would use even stronger means to condemn errors and horrors, if I did not fear thereby to make things worse. We have to have a lot of prudence in choosing our words. With prudence and patience, always joined together with the just affirmation of principles, one can save peoples and above all the innocent from an even worse catastrophe in this sad and frightening hour."

His job was, therefore, at the same time one of sagacity and of firmness, of equilibrium and of just moderation, a wonderful work that saved not only Rome but also a good part of humanity from a worse ruin.

I end this brief discussion of the public activity of that great Pontiff with the finely carved words which Domenico Cardinal Tardini pronounced in his commemorative address on October 20, 1959 in the Hall of Benedictions in the Vatican, before the Sacred College and a select audience.

> In a truly tragic world situation, Pius XII was called, as indeed he was, its *master*, but in reality he was at the same time its first victim.
>
> He, who was the most *afflicted* of all, became the *consoler* of all.
>
> He was the animator and drawer of crowds, but his truest and deepest yearning was for study, meditation, and solitude.
>
> An expert speaker, he seemed to delight in his polished and solid eloquence. Yet each one of those discourses and messages cost him long and painful labor.
>
> A wise guide, he often pointed out the right path to others, while not rarely he came upon so many difficulties in tracing out his own.
>
> His timid temperament caused him to shrink naturally from conflict. Nonetheless, he proved to be a fearless warrior every time that the protection of truth and justice and the welfare of souls required it.
>
> For this reason, Pius XII will go down in history as a Pontiff who was concurrently a wise reformer and a daring innovator.
>
> This whole complex of contrasts and contradictions sheds light on what I would call the mystery of Pius XII.
>
> Whoever does not understand all of this will never be able to appreciate the value of his chief merits and the perfection of his greatest virtues, a perfection which, it

is well to note, was achieved gradually, after much sweat and labor.

A grace was granted to those who remained near to Pius XII over the years, the grace to be present at his spiritual ascent, to see him continually rise higher, all the while becoming purer, thinner, more courteous, more magnificent.

In the end, the flame of his charity, having burned away the tiniest impurities of human frailty, poured forth and diffused throughout the whole world the rays and beams of heaven.

3. PIUS XII ENCOURAGES ME TO WRITE THE ITALIAN-LATIN DICTIONARY OF MODERN WORDS

Every once in a while when I am summoned to an audience with the Holy Father, I feel a sense of veneration and emotion as if a supernatural event were taking place. And indeed, is it not supernatural that after so many centuries, after so much history, and after so many often tempestuous events, Peter has survived in this man who represents Jesus Christ himself on earth, the foundation stone on which, by his will, his one Church is founded, whose pastor of pastors he is, and to whom is entrusted the whole flock, with no exception, and who is the vital and dynamic center of a spiritual kingdom that will experience storms, for sure, but never shipwreck, because it is meant to spread throughout all nations right up to the end of time?

It was with this sense of profound veneration that I used to enter an audience with Pius XII, and I still have before my eyes that thin figure, the penetrating gaze, the refined habits and the extreme courtesy.

I remember that when I used to enter and kneel down before him, he always smiled and said, "Please forgive me for bothering you. Sit down. Sit down." Then, when he gave me the work I had to do, he never used a word of command, but always asked if I would like to do him the favor of doing this or that, and he always ended by begging my pardon if he made me work too much. Such delicacy and refinement in dealing with people moved me.

In the first year of his pontificate, while he was at Castel Gandolfo for a bit of rest, which in reality was intense work, he summoned me to put his first encyclical into Latin. He had been composing it in those days, and he gave me twelve pages at a time, as soon as he had written them. I knew that he wanted to publish it as soon as possible, and therefore I tried to hurry the work along as best I could.

One day, I went to Castel Gandolfo with my twelve completed pages, but the Holy Father had not had the time to compose the twelve following ones. As soon as he saw me, he said, "How did you do it so quickly? I, on the other hand, have fallen behind."

"But Holy Father," I answered smiling, "Your Holiness has plenty of other things to attend to constantly."

"That's true, that's true," he added. "Still, I wouldn't have let you tire yourself so. How did you do it so fast?"

"I have the habit, Holy Father, when I have urgent business to attend to, to get up at 3:30 or 4:00 in the morning."

"Oh no! You shouldn't do that. That will ruin your health. Work instead in the evening after supper. I am used to working ordinarily until 2 AM. One works so much better at night when everything around you is quiet and no one bothers you."

"Thank you for your advice, Holy Father, but I couldn't do it that way. I don't have any problems in getting up and working in the early morning."

"Well, then, do as you see fit," His Holiness concluded, smiling. "Still, I wouldn't like to tire you out so much."

Pius XII really did make one work a lot. He, despite being so thin, was tireless, and his assistants had to be the same. But one worked well and gladly with him, for he was an inimitable example of tact, courtesy, and industry.

Very rarely he would make some observations about Latin to me, and when that happened, he spoke not only with delicacy, but with hesitation, with fear, as if begging my pardon. He would then grab Georges' *Latin-German Lexicon*, which he always had within reach, take a quick look, and then say, smiling, "OK, OK, you're right."

Probably no Pope, Leo XIII alone excepted, wrote so many documents of such importance and with so many implications as did

In the Service of Pius XII (1939-1958)

Pius XII: encyclicals, apostolic letters and constitutions, consistorial and extra-consistorial allocutions, messages, and radio addresses on every type of subject, even the most complicated and difficult.

With respect to Latin discourses, I recall an episode that illustrates his iron memory, comparable to that of Pico della Mirandola.

I had composed in haste (which was against his explicit instructions) an extremely long Latin discourse which the Holy Father was to pronounce shortly before a large audience in the Courtyard of San Damaso. I myself was at this audience. He began to recite this long discourse without the manuscript in his hands, as if he were improvising as he was going along.

I was astounded, and when, a few days afterwards, I had the occasion to be summoned to an audience to draft some papers, I could not do without expressing my wonder at what had happened. But he, smiling, said, "You know, by the grace of God, when I read a discourse three times, even if it is in Latin, I can easily recite it from memory. What is more, perhaps it escaped your notice that while I was reciting that speech, I skipped over a section that appeared too long to me, given that very few can understand classical Latin when they hear it, unless they know what to expect."

I replied that I had indeed noticed it, but that the speech went well enough even with that omission. "That's true, that's true," he added. "When it is published, the whole text will come out, and everyone can read it and be able to understand it more readily. But, you see, when I have to give a speech, even if it has been prepared and written up, after I have read it three times, I can skip whole paragraphs without losing my place because it is just as if I had the pages and paragraphs actually written before the eyes of my memory. That's not to my credit; it's a gift from God."

Among the many documents of Pius XII, there are not a few that deal with quite modern topics, and which therefore, when written up in Latin, require new terms. These terms belong to two categories, words which deal with modern things or inventions (there are very many of these), and new ideas which have risen from the progressive evolution of thought and the refinement of our sensibility. These last, which are perhaps the most difficult to translate into good

Latin, have been in great part introduced by Christianity, through that great upheaval and renewal of the human spirit that brought about so much ferment and new life. Let me give the following examples: spirit of sacrifice, spirit of humility and of self-denial, to deny oneself, to purify one's passions and transform them into virtues, to mortify one's *ego*, altruism, the social function of property, automation, communism, socialism, to socialize, socialization, totalitarianism, cult of the state, etc.

Naturally I had to try to translate all these phrases and thoughts in all their different senses into *classical* Latin, because such was the wish of Pius XII, who was a cultivated humanist and, I should say, quite scrupulous in the matter of purity of language.

Already in the reign of Pius XI I had had to draft in Latin the encyclical *Vigilanti Cura* on motion pictures, and later, under Pius XII, *Miranda Prorsus*, which was more complete in that it dealt with a variety of media, particularly radio, television, and cinematography.

I thus began to wonder whether it would be useful and timely to compose an *Italian-Latin Dictionary of Modern Words*. The work was not easy; however, it appeared necessary, especially for me, for which it was an indispensable tool of work. It was first necessary for me to brush up by reading all the Latin classics, even those of the Christian period; then I went on to the humanists, the epigraphists, and finally that most rich mine of Latinity, the *Acta Leonis*.

Before beginning, I asked the advice of the Holy Father, Pius XII, who not only encouraged me to undertake this work, but also told me that right from that moment on, he would be blessing my undertaking.

The fourth edition of this *Italian-Latin Dictionary of Modern and Difficult-to-Translate Words* appeared in 1963; it was published by *Editrice Studium* of Rome and consisted of 846 pages, each with two columns, on which about 12,000 words were considered and translations proposed. It was also enriched with various modern terms which had been collected and examined by my gallant colleagues of *Latinitas, Palaestra Latina*, and other similar publications during the last ten years. A long time ago, the humanists worked worthily to enlarge the domain of Latin to help it adapt to modern requirements and new needs. Writers of inscriptions worked to the same end, and among them S. A. Morcelli is worthy of special mention, for he produced the famous *Morcelli Lexicon of Inscriptions*, which was published by Filippo Schiassi. In more recent times, other works, of lesser value, have been completed, all, however, worthy of praise for the noble and useful goal which motivated their authors.

I don't pretend that my *Dictionary* is without defects, gaps, or inevitable omissions; for this reason I tried, as my friends and competent scholars advised, to perfect and enrich it more and more. One critic complained that there were occasionally exceptionally long circumlocutions. That's for sure, but one can't always translate new words and phrases by just one word, unless one wants to fall into the Latin style of Folengo, as Renzo has done. Circumlocutions can often be inserted into a sentence in such a clear, natural, and unobtrusive manner that all ponderousness and prolixity are removed. It's a question of knowing how to do it, and in any case the *Dictionary* cannot teach or suggest everything. It would be quite something if one could write good Latin just by having a dictionary in one's hand.

Horace, in his *Ars Poetica*, not only allows poets to introduce prudently, when necessary, new words, which derive, with a slight deviation (*parce detorta*) from a Grecian source, but also advises them to join words together in order to render new ideas. (*Dixeris, egregie, notum si callida verbum reddiderit iunctura novum*: A skillful arrangement may be able to give a new air and cast to old words.)

This is what I tried to do, and it is not for me to judge whether or not I succeeded. In any case, I can say that this book of mine, which required the most exhausting labor, has had a good press and has been read far and wide.

4. THE LAST DAYS OF PIUS XII

Advancing age and an ever more burdensome load of daily work began in time to take their toll on the health of Pius XII.

He used to spend long periods at the pontifical villa of Castel Gandolfo to enjoy a bit of refreshment and rest. But he did not find rest there, because the sense of his responsibility kept him working, and even when he went out for his usual brief walk, whether up at the pontifical villa or in the Vatican Gardens, he always carried with him the pages of some important document and made his rounds reading and thinking.

It therefore happened that after various bouts with illness, which he more or less overcame, the final catastrophe struck in the autumn of 1958 at the villa of Castel Gandolfo.

I still remember the immense void that all felt on that day; I recall the triumphant return of the corpse to the Vatican Basilica between two walls of mourning people, who wanted to give their last farewell to him who had been the *Pastor Angelicus*, the *Defensor Civitatis*, the tireless herald of peace.

This time too, as Secretary of Briefs to Princes, I had the duty of composing the funeral eulogy of the late Pontiff.

I now present this and my other compositions, which were the final tribute of lasting veneration which his Latin Secretary presented to the Pope.

PIUS XII PONT. MAX.

Eugenius Maria Iosephus Pacelli postr. cal. Mart. A. MDCCCLXXVI terrae caeloque natus est; paucas enim post horas quam mortalis huius vitae lucem aspexit, lustrali est sacri fontis aqua expiatus.

Inde a iuvenili aetate mentis acie, innocentia vitae, pietate impensissima erga Deum eiusque Virginem Matrem enituit.

In Viscontiano Lycio litteris ac liberalibus disciplinis tam alacrem dedit operam, ut praeceptorum laudibus honestaretur et condiscipulis omnibus praeluceret.

Cum divino quodam instinctu ad sacerdotium se vocatum agnosceret, in sacras adipiscendas doctrinas summo studio incubuit, ac postr. cal. Apr. a. MDCCCLXXXXIX ad hanc excelsam dignitatem est evectus.

In Sacrum Consilium Extraordinariis Ecclesiae Negotiis Procurandis cooptatus, tam citato gressu hoc in sibi credito munere fungendo processit, ut non multos post annos ab actis eiusdem Sacri Consilii esset, magna cum omnium aestimatione ipsiusque Pontificis Maximi Pii X praeconio.

Sancti huius Pontificis Successor Benedictus XV eum Archiepiscopali dignitate auxit, atque Apostolicum in Bavaria Nuntium delegit ac nominavit.

Qua in non facili provincia pactum conventum, quod "Concordatum" dicitur, inter Apostolicam Sedem hujusque regionis moderatores, ejus consilio, labore et opere feliciter sancitum est.

Anno autem MCMXXIX, cum iam in Germania Nuntium Apostolicum per aliquot annos egisset, cumque ibi ad aliam eiusdem generis eiusdemque gravitatis pactionem operam dedisset sapientissimam, a Summo Pontifice Pio XI Purpuratorum Patrum laticlavio decoratus est; ac duos tantum post menses Cardinalis a Publicis Ecclesiae Negotiis nominatus.

Decem post annos idem Pontifex piisime decessit e vita; ac bravissimo Cardinalium coetu habito, Eugenius Pacelli ad Summi Pontificatus apicem evectus est. Et quamvis iam in omnes fere populos calamitosum ruinosumque ingrueret bellum, hic tamen nuntius totius catholici orbis excitavit laetitiam; atque omnium oculi, mentes animique ad eum qui divino nutu in saeva illa tempestate Petrianae navis gubernacula moderabatur, nova luce perculsi novaque spe permoti, erecti sunt.

Graves, ac timoris, cladis ruinarumque pleni, elapsi sunt anni. Inter armorum clamorem, quae e terra, e mari, e caelo jacebantur, dum hominum communitas odio simultateque dilacerabatur, dum discordia fere ubique imperabat, dum divina in multorum animis languebat caritas, dum florentes denique urbes dirutae erant, ac valida juventus fraterno scelere necabatur, unus e Vaticana arce ad amorem, ad concordiam, ad pacem, quae vera pax esset, componendam adhortabatur omnes. Ac non est qui ignoret candidam Pii XII vestem innocenti cruore tum purpuratam esse, cum Romana ipsa Urbs, ignovomis e caelo verberata globis, diruta esset, et conclamantes multitudines Angelicum stiparent Pastorem, opem supernumque afferentem solacium.

Postea tacuere arma; sed odia, sed dissensiones, sed discordiae non siluere.

Oportebat imprimis sanare animos, diuturna simultate sauciatos; oportebat imprimis gliscentes profligare errores, et collustrare mentes divinis veritatibus.

In arduo hoc opere exsequendo Pius XII totus fuit. Sapientissimis enim editis documentis, et orationibus habitis paene innumeris, ad rectam amplectendam doctrinam, ad pacem, ad concordiam advocavit omnes. Praeterea sacra Iubilaea duo in catholico orbe celebranda indixit: alterum anno MCML, alterum autem primo exeunte saeculo, ex quo dogma Immaculatae Virginis Mariae ab eius Decessore fel. rec. Pio IX definitum fuerat. Atque, ut erat gerendarum rerum prudentia eximius, publicas in commune bonum inter Apostolicam Sedem ac Nationes plurimas conciliavit confirmavitque rationes necessitudinesque.

Sed tot tantisque curis laboribusque fractus, a.d. VII idus Oct., a. MCMLVIII, hora fere IV, complorantibus cuiusvis originis et cuiusvis religionis civibus ac gentibus, placidissimo obitu decessit.

Animo fuit leni ac miti, sed voluntate forti, invicta, tenacissima.

Effusa in pauperes caritate flagravit; ac nihil dulcius, suavius nihil habuit, quam egentium necessitatibus occurrere.

Evangelicam veritatem ac sacrosancta Ecclesiae iura, quae in non paucis Nationibus temerario ausu atque inhumanis prorsus insectationibus proculcabantur, iterum iterumque pro viribus tutatus est.

Vixit annos LXXXII, menses septem, dies septem.

Universae Ecclesiae praefuit annos XIX, menses septem, dies septem.

Ob eius obitum lux magna in terris restincta est; sed novum videtur in caelo refulgere sidus.

* * *

PIUS XII, SUPREME PONTIFF

Eugenio Maria Giuseppe Pacelli was born on earth and in heaven on March 2, 1876, for on the same day that he saw the light of this earthly life, he was reborn in the purifying waters of holy baptism.

Right from the earliest years of his youth he was distinguished by the sharpness of his intellect, by the innocence of his life, and by his intense devotion to God and the Most Holy Virgin Mary.

He enrolled at the Lyceum Visconti, where by his diligence and genius, he earned the praises of his teachers and excelled over his fellow students.

Then, feeling himself called from on high to the sacerdotal office, he zealously worked to acquire a deep and healthy religious education, and on April 2, 1899, he was elevated to the lofty dignity of the priesthood.

In the Service of Pius XII (1939–1958)

On account of his great merit, he was immediately summoned to serve in the first section of the Secretariat of State, whose secretary he was appointed not many years later by Pope St. Pius X, who held him in high esteem.

The successor of that saintly pontiff, Benedict XV, raised him to the archiepiscopal dignity and sent him to Bavaria as Apostolic Nuncio.

On account of his diligence, prudence, and tireless activity, an important concordat was concluded between the Holy See and Bavaria.

In 1929, Pope Pius XI elevated him to the honor of the sacred purple by creating him a cardinal, wishing in this way to reward the sensible performance of Msgr. Pacelli not only in Bavaria, but in all of Germany, where he had later been named Nuncio and had been able to conclude a new and important concordat.

About ten years later, when Pius XI had passed from earthly to eternal life, Eugenio Pacelli, after a short conclave, was raised to the pinnacle of the Supreme Pontificate. And even though the disastrous and ruinous Second World War was already evident on the horizon, this announcement brought joy to the whole Catholic world, and the eyes of all turned illuminated and full of new hope toward the bright figure of him who, in that turbulent hour, took in hand, in God's name, the helm of the prophetic bark of Peter.

Years full of horror, slaughter, and destruction followed. In the din of battle, which came from the land, the sea, and the air, while the human family was lacerated by hatred and ill-will, while discord prevailed almost everywhere because divine charity had grown weak in so many souls, while flourishing cities were reduced to rubble, and while able-bodied youths were mowed down by the arms of their brothers, he alone, the Pope, from the hill of the Vatican, called on all passionately to let love, harmony, truth, and genuine peace establish themselves once again. There is no one who does not know how the white cassock of Pius XII was rendered purple with the blood of innocents, for, when Rome herself was bombed, he entered fearlessly into the fiery ruins to bring help and comfort to the people, who surrounded their shepherd crying and screaming.

Then, finally, the arms were silent, but not hate, dissension, and discord.

It was above all necessary to calm and heal souls wounded by the daily rancor, and it was just as necessary to condemn errors and enlighten minds with divine truths.

Pius XII, at the war's end, dedicated himself entirely to these exalted tasks. By publishing the most wise documents, and by addressing almost innumerably many discourses and radio messages to the world, he summoned all to correct teaching, to peace, and to concord. He proclaimed two sacred jubilees for the Catholic world, one in 1950, the other at the end of the centenary of the definition of the dogma of the Immaculate Conception of the Virgin Mary proclaimed by his predecessor of happy memory, Pius IX. He was outstanding in the carefulness with which he conducted public affairs; he concluded many concordats between the Holy See and the nations, all the while maintaining the principles and prerogatives of the Church.

Finally, weakened by so great and tireless work, he was struck down with a grave illness, and on October 9, 1958, about 4 AM, he peacefully died to the regret of all.

His spirit was meek and delicate, but his will was brave, invincible, and most tenacious.

To the poor he showed the most generous charity, and he found nothing so sweet and pleasing as meeting public and private needs with munificence.

He oftentimes bravely defended the principles of the Gospel and the most holy laws of the Church, which, in many nations, were being deceitfully trampled down or even foolishly denied.

He lived 82 years, 7 months, and 7 days.

He was supreme head of the Catholic Church for 19 years, 7 months, and 7 days.

At his death, a great light went out on earth, but a new and bright star appeared in heaven.

* * *

The Most Illustrious and Most Reverend Lord Antonio Bacci, Secretary for Briefs to Princes, composed the following four elegiac poems for the base of the monument of the late pontiff.

I.

CVM. POPVLOS. FERE. OMNES
FORMIDOLOSVM. VEXARET. BELLVM
VNVS. EXSTITIT. SINCERAE. PACIS
CONCILIATOR
VRBIS. DEFENSOR
AERVMNOSORVM. SOLATOR
STVDIOSISSIMVS

II.

INSVRGENTES. ERRORES
INVICTA. ANIMI. FORTITVDINE
COMPESCVIT. PROFLIGAVIT
FILIOS. AVTEM. ABERRANTES
AD. PATERNVM. REVOCAVIT
AMPLEXVM
VERITATEM. FACIENS. IN. CARITATE

III.

PASTOR. ANGELICVS
SIBI. CREDITVM. GREGEM
AD. AETERNAE. VITAE. PASCVA
INDEFATIGABILI. CVRA
PERDVXIT

IV.

PENTECOSTIS. MVNERE. QVASI
PRAEDITVS. ORATOR
VI. SENTENTIARVM. PERSPICVVS
SVBTILITATE. ACVTVS
MAGNILOQVENTIA. GRANDIS
CVIVSVIS. LINGVAE. GENTES
AD. RECTE. SENTIENDVM
VIVENDVMQVE. PERMOVIT

* * *

I.

While a horrible war
consumed almost every nation
he alone was the promoter of a true peace
the Defender of the City
the most zealous consoler of the miserable.

II.

Through the invincible bravery of his soul
he checked and routed raging errors,
but his erring children
he called back to his paternal embrace
combining truth with charity.

III.

The Angelic Pastor
led with tireless attention
the flock entrusted to his care
to the pastures of eternal life.

IV.

An orator gifted with the charism of Pentecost
he was clear in the meaning of his sentences
keen in the art of exactness.
Preeminent in eloquence
he motivated people of every language
to think right and to live right.

IV
In the Service of John XXIII (1958-1963)

1. A MEETING WITH MSGR. RONCALLI

It was only twenty years ago that I first had the occasion to converse with Msgr. Roncalli, who at that time was Apostolic Delegate in Turkey. Before then I had only met him and greeted him during the frequent trips he made to Rome on business.

I was at Castel Gandolfo in the Pontifical Antechamber waiting for an audience. I recall that I was tired and preoccupied with an important papal document which I had in my hands and had already been working on for several months, but it had not yet attained that full perfection of thought and that precision of form which the Holy Father desired.

While I waited for my turn to be summoned to the audience, I saw Msgr. Roncalli come in; he immediately greeted me with that open and smiling countenance of his. Then, seeing that I was preoccupied, he asked me in his good-natured manner, "It looks to me as if you have something on your mind. Have courage. Look at me. I've been called back from the East for God knows what destination, but I think that I am in God's hands, and whatever He wants will certainly be for my good and for the good of the Holy See. We are in good hands, dear friend, in the hands of Providence. So, have courage; you will see that everything will come out for the best."

I looked at him with admiration, and thanked him for his good and friendly words, which I took into the depths of my heart.

A little bit later I went in for my audience, and all in fact did go quite well. I came out with my serenity restored. Msgr. Roncalli, who was scheduled to go in after me, saw me smiling, and seemed to take pleasure in my happiness.

2. GOOD POPE JOHN

When, after the death of Pius XII, the conclave for the election of the new Pope opened, I once again had the obligation to compose and recite before the Sacred College of Cardinals the *Oratio de Eligendo Pontifice* (Speech for the Election of the Pope), as I had done at the death of Pius XI, for I was still the Latin Secretary of Briefs to Princes. I recall that my speech, or rather exhortation, to the electors of the new Pope was well received, even in the press. Someone wrote that in my discourse I had clearly and precisely drawn a portrait of John XXIII.

In reality, I had merely discussed before the cardinals the *ideal figure* of the Supreme Pontiff that the times required. It was not thanks to me if the newly elected pontiff corresponded to this ideal in the highest degree, just as my sermon had delineated him.

Since John XXIII was elected Pope in an evening scrutiny, I had to meet with him late into the night, just as I had done after the election of Pius XII, in order to help him compose his Latin radio message which he had to address to the whole world on the following morning. I found the new Pope serene and tranquil, just as I had seen him years before at Castel Gandolfo in the Pontifical Antechamber before my audience. It was that full and complete serenity that only absolute faith and total abandonment to the will of God can give.

Goodness and serenity were certainly the most conspicuous endowments of John XXIII, a simple goodness and a complete serenity, which surely sprang from his profound interior spirituality.

The people called him John the Good, the parish priest of the world. Everyone wished him well, and I think that even the dissidents were at a loss as to what evil to speak of him, and they spoke no evil of him precisely because they were sure that it would be counterproductive, since the Pope was loved and venerated by all.

When, at noon, he appeared at the window of his private apartment to bless the crowd that filled St. Peter's Square, all eyes would look up at the good Pope as soon as he made his harmonious and paternal voice heard, and all their hearts would start beating in unison. I remember one day, it was Christmas, when I too was in the crowd. The Pope appeared, recited the *Angelus* with the people in the square, and then, opening his paternal heart with his loveable simplicity, said, "Merry Christmas, dear children, Merry Christmas! Bring my blessing to everybody, to everybody. And you parents, when you go home, give a kiss and a hug for me to your children. Tell them that it is a kiss and a hug from the Pope."

Profoundly moved, I looked around and could see that many had tears in their eyes, tears of joy.

In that marvelous book entitled *Journal of a Soul*, an incomparable and inexhaustible treasure of that interior spirituality whence all the exterior activity of Pope John XXIII spontaneously sprang forth, there are pages that fully describe the simple, candid, and good soul of that great pontiff. Let me cite a few:

> Being simple and unpretentious costs me nothing. It's a great grace which the Lord has given me. I want to continue being worthy of it.

And against cunning, the worst product of the human mind, he wrote:

> I leave excessive cunning and so-called diplomatic skill to everybody else and continue to content myself with my good nature and simplicity of sentiment, word, and deed.

One shouldn't think, however, that this good nature and simplicity of his didn't have its own particular skill and unique shrewdness, circumspection, and prudence. In fact, he used to like to quote frequently, applying them to himself, the words of St. John Chrysostom: *Hoc est philosophiae culmen: simplicem esse cum prudentia.* ("The height of philosophy is to be simple prudently.")

During a spiritual retreat in preparation for his eightieth birthday, when he was already, perhaps, beginning to feel the first symptoms of his grave illness, he wrote, among other things:

As this spiritual retreat of mine comes to an end, I clearly perceive the real substance of the task which Jesus, either permitting or disposing, has entrusted to my life.

Vicarius Christi? I am not worthy of that title, I, the poor son of Battista and Marianna Roncalli, two good Christians for sure, but so modest and humble. *Vicarius Christi*, well, that means my job is to be *sacerdos et victima*, priest and victim. The priesthood elevates me, but the sacrifice, which the priesthood brings to mind, makes me tremble.

Blessed Jesus, God and man! I renew my consecration to you for life, for death, and for eternity.

From looking at what happens in life and what is going on around me, I am naturally led to stop frequently on Calvary, there to converse both with Jesus as he lies dying and with his mother, and thence to come down to his holy tabernacle, his resting place in the sacrament.

3. PONTIFICAL SPEECHES AND DOCUMENTS

The discourses of John XXIII were often an improvised, spontaneous, and paternal conversation; they had the style of a nice talk, in which his interior spirituality and the warmth of his good soul and great heart were reflected and made to shine. This was why they were pleasing, attractive, and moving. In his private audiences, his amiability and sweetness seemed even nearer and more pleasing.

I recall, among others, the following certain episodes.

One day he said to me, "I always get up at four in the morning; that's my hour."

"That's too soon," I replied timidly. "Even Your Holiness needs rest."

"Yes, that's true; I need rest, but I need work too," he replied, smiling. "What's more, you can pray so much better in the morning, at first light, when the whole world is quiet. I'm accustomed to say three rosaries, and except in those early morning hours, I wouldn't easily be able to find the necessary time and opportunity for concentration."

In the Service of John XXIII (1958-1963)

"As for myself, Holy Father," I joined in, "I only say one."

"That's OK, but you're not the Pope. I, who am Pope, have so many responsibilities and so great a need of divine assistance, that I have to pray a lot more than you, wouldn't you say so?"

In another audience, which followed upon my having offered him my book of daily meditations (*Meditazioni per tutti i giorni dell'anno*, Marietti, Torino 1959), he greeted me smiling and said right away, "Do you know that I have been using your beautiful book when I make my meditations? It's perfect for me."

I was confused about what to say and replied, "Holy Father, thank you for these kind words, but my small book of meditations is quite a poor, simple thing."

"And it's precisely on account of its simplicity that I like it so much," the Pope replied, smiling once again. "I'm simple too. Up to now I've been using an old manual of meditations, good and substantial, but too abstract and complicated. Instead of doing me much good, it made me tired. Your book, it's true, I find simple, but also intimate, spontaneous. That's why I like it."

John XXIII was noteworthy not only for his great goodness, amiability, and simplicity, but also for the important Pontifical documents he issued. I should mention especially his first encyclical, *Ad Petri Cathedram*, which announced his program, and two others, *Mater et Magistra* and *Pacem in Terris*. These encyclicals had a quite widespread and beneficial impact worldwide.

Even in this regard I have a personal reminiscence which may be related without giving away any state secret.

Whenever the Pope entrusted me with writing up some particularly important Pontifical document, he used to have a long talk with me, which sometimes lasted for over an hour.

This happened even if it was merely a matter of making some minor modifications or additions to a document that had already been put into Latin. Above all, he desired that nothing unpleasant remain that anyone could find polemic, or irritating, but instead that the spirit of goodness, charity, and amiability, which he loved so much and which was his natural characteristic, shine through in everything.

He used to say that there have always been those who have shown themselves by word or deed to be enemies of the Church, but that the Church itself did not have enemies, only children, to whom it wished well, like a mother, and whom it tried to help in the best way possible.

He was especially saddened by the secret, treacherous, and technically perfect manner in which the Church was persecuted in certain nations where the bishops and priests were impeded in the free exercise of their ministry, and where the fundamental freedoms of the human being, even those which are considered inalienable in our modern times and culture, are all too often trampled upon; nevertheless, even in cases such as these he preferred the path of persuasion, exhortation, love, and especially prayer to the path of outright condemnation, which, however, he did not fail to take, and that quite clearly, whenever necessary.

4. THE SECOND VATICAN COUNCIL

The name of John XXIII will forever remain linked with the convocation of the Second Vatican Council. It was an act of great courage, the courage of one who sees everything from the point of view of Deity and who determines to move ahead in spite of obstacles and difficulties.

The Council of Trent had finished about four centuries previously, and many things had become old fashioned, and times had changed.

The First Vatican Council, as is well known, had to end abruptly, when there was still much to do and still grave problems to resolve. There was a feeling in the Church that it was time for an updating, not of dogmas, which belong to the sacred and immutable deposit entrusted by Christ to the hierarchical magisterium, which legitimately protects and interprets it in strict union with the Pope, but of ecclesiastical structures, a renewal required by the passing of time and by cultural and social necessities, though even then only after an attentive, accurate, and prudent examination.

It was like (and so it appeared to all) a great window opened up to let the sun shine on the world, and everyone understood that the grand assembly wanted and indeed had to address that profound anxiety about unity and peace that especially today agitates and concerns all, even the brethren separated from the See of Peter, who, divided among themselves and from Rome, must hear the supreme invitation of Christ, *Ut omnes unum sint* (John XVII, 21), that all may be one, as well as his unforgettable prediction and prophecy *Et fiet unum ovile et unus pastor*, and there will be one flock and one shepherd (John X, 16).

5. A BED THAT IS AN ALTAR

The work of the Council had scarcely begun when a grave illness struck the Pope who had desired it, inspired it, and organized it. He nonetheless did not lose courage but serenely remained at his post, praying, spurring the Council on, and tiring himself beyond his ability to recuperate, which was now worn out by an inexorable malady. Surely he offered his life for the happy and fruitful outcome of the Council.

When the word spread about that the Pope was gravely ill, everyone felt profoundly anxious and sorrowful. All prayed, even non-Christians and people of no religion whatsoever.

Inquiries came in from all over the world and from all classes of people, but the news was ever sadder and more discomforting.

The good Pope suffered in an attitude of complete and serene resignation, faith, and love, and kept on praying for all his children, blessing every one of them.

With his eyes turned to the crucifix which hung directly across from his bed, he prayed as follows right before he died:

> This bed is an altar; the altar requires a victim. Here I am. I offer my life for the Church, for the continuation of the Ecumenical Council, for the peace of the world, and for love among Christians.
>
> The secret of my priesthood rests in the Crucified One, whom I wanted to be placed in front of my bed. He guides me, and I speak to Him. During long and frequent nighttime conversations, the thought of the redemption of the world appeared to me more urgently

than ever. *Et alias oves habes, quae non sunt ex hoc ovili.* (And you have other sheep, which are not of this fold.) Those outstretched arms say that He died for all, for all. No one is refused His love or His pardon.

In this last hour, I feel tranquil, and I feel certain that My Lord, in His mercy, will not reject me. As unworthy as I am, I wanted to serve Him, and I have tried to do nothing other than render homage to the truth, to justice, to charity, to the *mitis et humilis corde* (meek and humble of heart) of the Gospel.

My life on earth is over, but Christ lives, and the Church goes on with its work. The souls, the souls . . . *ut unum sint, ut unum sint . . .*

The good Pope then died peacefully, to universal lamentation, on June 3, 1963.

V
In The Service of Paul VI

1. HABEMUS PAPAM!
There is a popular saying *Whoever enters the conclave Pope, comes out Cardinal.* This means that human arrangements made at the beginning of the conclave often come to nothing.

This proverb, however, could not be applied to the conclave that put Paul VI on the pontifical throne, for the whole world press had been predicting as the most probable successor of John XXIII, Giovanni Battista Cardinal Montini, Archbishop of Milan.

When, after a conclave of a day and a half, Alfredo Cardinal Ottaviani, the Senior Cardinal Deacon, pronounced from the external balcony of the Vatican Basilica the solemn words, *"Habemus Papam, Joannem Baptistam Montini...,"* there was an outburst of uncontrollable enthusiasm from the piazza below and from the colonnades on the sides. Everybody was expecting that name; everybody was expecting that Pope.

It seemed to all to be predestined by providence; it seemed to all that an invisible hand had guided him step by step to the pontifical throne. Substitute of the Secretariat of State for many years, then Pro-Secretary of State, he knew as few others know the complex organization of the Church and of the Roman Curia. Archbishop of one of the biggest and most important dioceses of Italy, he had further been able to acquire a long experience in pastoral ministry, wherein he labored with an open mind and tireless zeal for not a few years. He therefore appeared to be, as he certainly is, a complete Pope.

He unites the perspicacity and sure and tested intuition of Pius XII with the great heart, the goodness, the finesse in dealing with people, and the apostolic spirit of John XXIII. The very name he has assumed, with clear reference to the Apostle of the Gentiles, indicates his all-encompassing and comprehensive design, open to all, and his apostolic dynamism.

After scarcely a year, he has acquired the admiration and veneration of everyone. An indefatigable worker, a man of vast culture and wide experience, a priest of sensitive and deep piety, he has quickly grasped the helm of the Church with a sturdy grip, and guides it forwards, not backwards, according to the words spoken by Christ to St. Peter, the first Pope: *Duc in altum*, Launch out into the deep (Luke v, 4).

2. THE CONTINUATION OF THE COUNCIL

His predecessor had left him a great and weighty legacy, the Ecumenical Council. But he entered sure-footed, serenely, and with firm will through the door opened to the light from the heart of John XXIII.

This grand event in the life of the Church, towards which the eyes and hopes of so many, indeed, of all, turn, truly requires the presence of a Pope of an exceptional disposition and of extraordinary gifts, and this disposition and these gifts are fully in evidence in the intelligence, heart, and will of Paul VI, especially in his firm and decisive will, which is surely a great gift from God.

It has been said that some serious disagreements have arisen among the Council Fathers, right from the first session. But one must understand this: probably never, no, certainly never, has the ecclesiastical hierarchy enjoyed such concord and such full harmony both in defending the sacred deposit of Christ's doctrine entrusted to the Church and in submitting unconditionally to the Vicar of Christ on earth.

There have certainly been differences of opinion, as one would have in any free debate, but these have never been about doctrine or defined dogma, but rather about the best and most suitable way of expressing this doctrine and presenting it in the most perfect terms possible, so that on the one hand, no dangerous ambiguities should arise, and on the other hand, people today would best be able to understand them; furthermore, these terms must take into account the currents of thought and the particular conditions that prevail in our times.

This is what the conciliar debate is all about; it is not at all a matter of discussing dogmas and much less of changing them, but only of illustrating them better and rendering them more understandable and more agreeable to the thought and the age in which we live.

3. THE GOODNESS AND FRIENDLINESS OF THE PONTIFF

If the profound gaze and open mind of Paul VI immediately win over the mind and earn the admiration of whoever approaches him, his heart and his finesse in dealing with people quickly attract their sympathy and veneration.

I shall always remember the first audience that I had right after his election. He came up to me and embraced me as if he were embracing his brother, his friend. And when I brought him the fourth edition of my *Italian-Latin Dictionary of Modern and Difficult-to-Translate Words*, he spoke with me in such a friendly way that I remained profoundly moved. But there is more; the next day an autograph letter from him arrived, in which he wrote these words:

> Our admiration for such a learned work is joined together with the wish that the noble and current use of the Latin language, to which the Church even today still owes the clearness, vigor, and integrity of her official documents, may derive from it the widest utility.

Since I became a cardinal in the last years of John XXIII and was therefore no longer Latin Secretary of Briefs to Princes, my service to the Popes has taken on a different nature; even though, once in a while, I am still invited, in exceptional cases, to help out in drawing up Pontifical documents, my major contribution now takes place in the four Sacred Congregations of which I am a member, the Sacred Congregation of the Council, the Sacred Congregation of Religious, the Sacred Congregation of Rites, and the Sacred Congregation of Seminaries and Universities.

What is more, I have made my contribution as a Council Father in the deliberations of Vatican II, as best as my limitations allow, by exhorting in particular that we avoid all imprecision and ambiguity of language, which, in such solemn and important acts, might generate confusion, damage, and danger.

4. THE TRIP TO PALESTINE

Paul VI conceived the pleasant idea of making an apostolic pilgrimage to the land of Jesus to visit the places made holy by the life, death, and glorious resurrection of the Redeemer, as if to signify thereby that we must all return to the living and vital roots of Christianity if we want the Gospel to produce spiritual renewal, peace, and unity of all in one faith and one love, in which we must all be as brothers under the indefectible guidance of a single shepherd.

This event made quite an impression on everybody; it was the first time that a Pope had returned the voyage that St. Peter, guided by the light of God, had made when he came from the east to the west, where he was to end his life as a martyr, leaving to his successors, the bishops of Rome, the mandate of Christ to nourish the whole Christian flock, to be the foundation stone of the Church, and to keep the keys of the Kingdom of Heaven, with the sure promise that everything that they loosed or bound on earth would be loosed or bound in heaven.

Paul VI's trip to Palestine appeared to be the prelude and hint of that Christian unity to come, which is the desire and concern of all, even those brothers of ours separated from the Apostolic See, and even those dissidents of the other Christian confessions.

May the Lord grant a happy and complete fulfillment to this prelude and this hope, a prelude and hope expressed in the emotional and moving prayer that Paul VI recited on Calvary, gathering together in his mind, in his heart, and in his words the supplication, the thought, and the entreaty of the whole of mankind.

VI
Latin and the Council

1. WHAT LANGUAGE IS USED AT THE COUNCIL, AND IN WHAT STYLE OF LATIN ARE THE CONCILIAR DOCUMENTS AND ACTS WRITTEN?

As the opening day of the Second Vatican Council drew near, the question arose: What language should be used for the deliberations of the Council? In February, 1962, I published the following ideas in the press.

The Constitution Veterum Sapientia

The solemnity with which the Supreme Pontiff John XXIII deigned to sign, in the important audience held in the Vatican Basilica on the Feast of Saint Peter's Chair, 1962, the apostolic constitution *Veterum Sapientia* for the increase in the study of Latin especially in seminaries and in Catholic schools, motivates me to return to the important issue of what language should be used at the Second Vatican Council.

In this matter, there have been advanced, by certain individuals, ideas which are not quite correct and which do not agree with the ancient tradition that was maintained even at the last Ecumenical Council held in 1870.

The Views of Fr. Dehon

While I was reading the *Diary of the First Vatican Council* by the Servant of God Leo Dehon (*Diario del Concilio Vaticano I* by Leo Dehon, edited by Vincenzo Carbone, Vatican Polyglot Press, 1962), I found, together with the high degree of spirituality that pervades those pages, certain observations that appear to me to be most opportune and worthy to be considered during the celebration of Vatican Council II.

Fr. Dehon served as the official stenographer at the sessions of that Council. Not only was he an inspired soul pervaded by a profound sense of *Romanità*, so much so that he affirmed, with St. Bridget, "Rome is the short-cut to heaven," but he was also a lively fellow, an acute observer of men and things, and a fair commentator on the events of his time.

Thus, he reproved, for example, the assertion of those who, on account of their excessive zeal, spoke of the work of the various preparatory commissions as a "Pre-Council" that would take away or reduce the Council Fathers' liberty of discussion. This may be recalled today when, in a magazine that is supposed to be taken seriously, they talk, once again, with regard to the *schemata* (drafts) prepared by the different Commissions and Secretariats, of a written Pre-Council, which will be succeeded by the oral Council. This accusation is not only inexact, but theologically false. According to Catholic doctrine, the gift of infallibility in matters of faith and morals belongs personally to the Pope and collegially to the Council Fathers in union with him. The aforementioned drafts, therefore, do not form a written Pre-Council, but merely enjoy whatever authority corresponds to the competence of the members and consultants who form the Commissions that composed them.

There are also certain pages in that *Diary* concerning the question of Latin and the way in which the conciliar debates were held in that language. First of all, Fr. Dehon writes explicitly and significantly:

> Without Latin, that vast assembly would have degenerated into a linguistic Tower of Babel. It was, in fact, on account of Latin that the prelates were able to get their ideas across easily. Of course, not everybody spoke with the same facility, but they were all able to be understood without difficulty... and were able to send back their reactions and comments in Latin to the Conciliar Commissions, which had taken the place of the Preparatory Commissions. Naturally, there were differences in pronunciation, and it often happened in the first days that the gravity of the Italian cardinals and bishops did not

prevent their bursting out in laughter when they heard the language of Cicero spoken with pronunciations to which their ears were not accustomed. Msgr. Pie wittily applied the words of Sacred Scripture to this variety of pronunciations: *Multifariam multisque modis olim Deus loquens patribus in prophetis* (Hebrews 1:1), and Msgr. Mermillod begged everyone's pardon, saying, "Though our pronunciation, Reverend Fathers, may be French, our hearts are Roman."

Fr. Dehon continues and says that "the English were notorious for their pronunciation," that the Germans were harsh and rough, that the Hungarians gargled, that the Spaniards pronounced *vivere* like *bibere*, that "the French did not shine in the elegance and correction of their Latinity," that grammatical mistakes were flying in from every direction, but that nevertheless everyone succeeded in getting himself understood; "*Peu importe, on se comprenait.*"

Linguistic Organization of the Council

I think that if at the First Vatican Council, all the Fathers spoke in Latin and succeeded in being understood without great difficulty, the same should be true at the Second Vatican Council.

In this matter, there are two quite distinct questions. Both, however, are very important; we are not dealing here with peripheral issues, like whether or not to drape the bright polychrome marbles of the Vatican Basilica with imitation tapestries; it is a question of giving an intelligible and worthy clothing both to the discussions of the Conciliar Fathers and, even more, to those documents containing the precepts and norms which the Ecumenical Council, after wise examination, deliberation, and approval, will promulgate. In my humble opinion, the two questions require at once not only a prudent and accurate examination, but also that some appropriate provisions be made.

Everyone knows that the study of Latin is everywhere in decline; one can discuss the causes and the remedies, but one thing is certain: a decline there surely is. This situation, which a recent circular letter of the Sacred Congregation of Seminaries and Universities, directed to the episcopate of the whole world, correctly recognizes, has spread most troublesomely even into the ranks of the clergy. From the clergy in general, this tendency to degenerate might well spread, God forbid, even to the Sacred Congregations of the Roman Curia, especially if those who are in charge of Latin in its various offices cannot find the wherewithal to increase the number of their Latinists and, what is more, to educate them not only with the word but by their personal example.

In short, what is necessary, in my modest opinion, is to increase the number of Latinists in the Curia and to give them that complete and practical formation which only experienced Latinists know how to give. It is not enough that they be intelligent, cultured, and skillful in other subjects; it is necessary to be such *in this particular subject*, so much the more because a good formation in Latin cannot be improvised in a few months or in a few years, but requires a long apprenticeship.

There are still some excellent Latinists in the Roman Curia, as I well know from direct experience, but they are few; I'm talking here of the small and courageous band that works in the two Latin secretariats of the Holy See. From this little company, and not from those who may have left Latin behind on their school desks, must come the masters of the Latin offices of the Curia, whom we need so much, especially today.

2. IN WHICH LANGUAGE?

The first question that I proposed, namely, what language should be spoken at the Second Vatican Council, might seem useless and out of place to some. Isn't Latin, in fact, the official language of the Church, lively recommended by the Supreme Pontiffs and the Code of Canon Law, and used even at the First Vatican Council? With good reason Benedict xv affirms that Latin is much more suited than modern languages to express the dogmas of the Church with faithfulness and precision, and Pius xi affirms as much, when he calls it "the Catholic language" (*quam dicere catholicam vere possumus*). And the Pontiff now gloriously reigning has many times exhorted the clergy in particular to study this language, which is the bond of communication and of unity among the different peoples who form the Church, the *vinculum unitatis*.

The vulgar languages are in continual change; often words do not have today the same meaning that they had yesterday, or at best have one meaning for one person and another meaning for someone else. About these terms we can truly say with Sallust, *Vera vocabula rerum amisimus* (*Catil.*, c. 52). We have lost the right words in these cases. However, the Latin language is not only the most organic and logical language that has ever existed, but, for the very fact that it is no longer spoken by the people, it is now fixed, precise, and unequivocal, and presents us with well defined technical terms which have already been consecrated by the Church as the fruit of long discussions and solemn definitions, terms which it would be dangerous to ignore.

By means of Latin, the Church can avoid that damaging linguistic Babel, which not rarely is the seed of misunderstandings and discord even in international gatherings.

All the same, in various places, especially in America, people have noted the grave difficulty that this problem presents today; some have even mentioned the possibility that in the Ecumenical Council, as in other great international congresses, for practical reasons one allow everyone to talk in his own language and then have it translated simultaneously by some system into other languages. There are two main difficulties with making Latin the sole language: first, the great trouble many Council Fathers have in speaking in Latin, and second, the not lesser difficulty everyone else has in understanding them, given the differences in pronunciation of this language in the various countries.

These difficulties were already noticed by the late Cardinal Secretary of State Domenico Tardini who, in a talk given on October 31, 1959 to representatives of the world press, used these wise words, which were quoted in the *L'Osservatore Romano* on the next day:

> As regards the language that will be used in the proceedings of the Council, it will be Latin, the language of the Church, since it is particularly suited to express precisely,

clearly, and concisely the concepts of doctrine and the norms of discipline. We are not for now thinking about simultaneous translations via headphones, because in matters of faith, one word poorly or even imprecisely translated might give rise to confusion.

A Plain and Scholastic Latin

One couldn't put it better; I fully understand that the two principal difficulties which people have put forward really do exist, but I insist that they are quite separate. On the one hand, to hold an Ecumenical Council in the various national languages with a system of cubicles and headphones would give the impression, if not of repudiating Latin as the official language of the Church, at least of making it one among many. Now is it at all possible that right at this very moment when, with great superficiality, some people are trying to reduce or banish outright the study of that wonderful language, which, together with Greek, is the natural womb of our civilization and of our literatures and which is still the sole linguistic bond among cultured people amidst such a variety of tongues, is it at all possible, I ask, that even the Church, which has always maintained, defended, and encouraged the study of Latin, should now repudiate or abandon it? In interviews, contacts, and even special meetings related to the Council, one might use other languages, but in the solemn sessions and general congregations, there is no doubt that the official language of the Church, Latin, must prevail.

One could get around the first difficulty in great measure by having recourse not to Classical Latin (which very few indeed would be able to speak), but to a plain, fluent, and flexible Latin, such as is ordinarily used in the documents of the Sacred Congregations, or even to that kind of Latin which we call *scholastic*, which is spoken and can be heard in the lecture halls of the Gregorian University and of other ecclesiastical universities, which are attended by a great number of students from almost all nations. If those professors can manage to be understood and those students to understand, why shouldn't the venerable Fathers of the Ecumenical Council not be able to do the same?

Surely there were not lacking at the Ecumenical Councils of Florence, Trent, and the Vatican Fathers who knew how to speak in the language of Cicero, renewed and brought back to life by the inspiration of Christianity. I recall having read with deep pleasure the inaugural address pronounced in elegant Latin by Archbishop Ragazzoni at the beginning of the Council of Trent; Archbishop Passavalli, himself from Trent, did not achieve the same heights when he made the inaugural address at the First Vatican Council. Yet it is good to hope that in our Council there will not be a complete lack of the best examples of a pure Latinity. This will give a necessary prestige to the Church before the learned of the world, who still cultivate the great humanistic traditions, but it would be unrealistic to require that everyone talk like that; a Council is not a literary academy. The language of the Fathers will have first of all to be scientific, precise, clear, and exact, and this is what scholastic Latin, which our Mediaeval doctors and modern professors of various ecclesiastical disciplines have studiously and wisely forged, so admirably offered.

In this respect, one must note that the Church, even in the matter of Latin, as in every other matter, is moved by higher and universal criteria; she has embraced and embraces Latin during all her varied and glorious history, and, according to different circumstances, needs, and classes of persons, she has used and continues to use that Latin, which is more fit for the purpose and for the intellectual formation of the people whom she addresses. In this way, it becomes possible, in my opinion, to use Latin even in an international gathering at which bishops and theologians from all nations come together.

Keep to the Roman Pronunciation

The second difficulty remains, that of the different pronunciations. It is known that the pronunciation of Latin, as that of every other language, has not always been the same. The pronunciation used today in the liturgy of the Church, which is customarily called the Roman pronunciation, is not that of the classical period, but rather that which came into use in the fourth century, that is, at the time of the great Fathers of the Latin Church. Such is the prevailing view among the learned today, though others claim that the classical pronunciation maintained itself for a further few centuries. But these latter rely on an inexact argument, namely, they rely on the fact that even after the fourth century the grammarians continued to teach the classical pronunciation. However, the traditional teaching of the grammarians is one thing, while the living usage of the people is another. In the age of Cicero, the pronunciation was quite different. The letters *c*, *g*, and *t*, for example, were then read as hard even before the letters *e* and *i*, and the diphthongs *ae* and *oe* were pronounced in a disarticulated fashion, that is, about as they are written. A little later, these sounds became softer and blurred, and as a result there emerged the pronunciation that is still in use today, not only in the Church, but even in the Italian schools, if we except the universities, where the classical pronunciation was introduced some time ago. It is not a matter of one being false and the other true; they are both true. They are like different photographs of the same person, one of him in his youth, the second in the fullness of his manhood, and the third in his old age.

There is a document of St. Pius X, a Pontifical Letter to the French Archbishop Louis Dubois (*Acta Apostolicae Sedis* 1912, p. 578), in which it is recommended that one continue to promote, not for critical or philological reasons, but for reasons of uniformity, the Roman pronunciation of Latin in the liturgy. The same point was made, though with greater vigor, by Pius XI in his letter to Cardinal Bisleti (*Acta Apostlicae Sedis* 1926, p. 302 ff.). It seems to me that these documents retain their full validity; thus, for reasons of uniformity and practicality, it is best that the Council Fathers stick to the aforementioned Roman pronunciation of Latin.

Finally, in order that the Press Office might operate in an opportune, timely, and precise manner, it is necessary that an adequate group of competent Latinists, attentively following the progress of the discussions among the Council Fathers, write up an exact summary in the various modern languages, a summary that can be dispensed to the various representatives of the press, lest these fellows make use of other sources of information that might be inexact and imprecise.

3. IN WHICH LATIN?

If, in replying to the first question, I held it necessary to follow quite wide criteria, because I considered them opportune for evident practical reasons, nevertheless, in responding to the second, namely, in what kind of Latin should the documents and acts of the Council be written, I believe it necessary to be somewhat strict, insofar as it seems to me that one should not relegate to oblivion the noble traditions of classical Latin, which flourished in the Roman Curia from the time of our best humanists and which were later on taken up again with renewed vigor by Leo XIII and the pontiffs who came after him.

If, in reading the acts of the Council of Trent and of Vatican I, we do not find the language of Cicero, we find before us nevertheless a decorous and clear Latin not without an elegance of its own. If the best Latinists did not write those documents, good Latinists certainly did. The results were drafts which, though not in an academic-literary style, were certainly worthy of those two great congresses of the Church universal.

If, now, we take in hand that golden volume produced by the Council of Trent, the *Catechismus ad parochos*, whose fourth section was composed by Giulio Cardinal Pogiani, the Pope's secretary, and whose previous sections were accurately revised by the same prelate, we see how the classical language of Rome can be perfectly harmonized with Christian thought, and how it docilely and nimbly, though without literary embellishments, accommodates itself so as to express those new thoughts and those new teachings which Christianity has bestowed on mankind.

Humanistic Latin and a Dignified and Decorous Latin

There have always been two contrasting parties among the Latin Secretaries of the Popes. The head of one was Bembo, a great humanist in the tradition of Cicero, but a man with a paganizing tendency, who repudiated that store of Christian words that are absolutely necessary to express the dogmas of our faith and who, writing to his friend Giacomo Sadoleto, dared to reprove him because, in his opinion, he was wasting his time writing a commentary on the letters of St. Paul, rendering barbarous with Christian terminology the golden tongue of Cicero. The other current had for its chief this same Cardinal Sadoleto, who, though also a polished and elegant Latinist, did not reject that linguistic treasury with which the Christian classics enriched and revived the ancient language of Rome. It is clear that the line followed by Sadoleto and pursued by many of his successors is that which should be followed today. It is obvious that one should not, on account of some false love of purity or classical elegance, call the Eucharist *crustulum salvificum* or refer to the Holy Trinity as *triforme numen*, but neither is it permissible to fall into the trap of producing a sort of pig-Latin, something that satisfies all requirements except that it is not Latin, but instead smacks of Italian, German, or English, and gives the horrible impression of a carpet turned upside-down.

It is necessary to resume the connection with and return to the noble traditions of our best and most sensible humanists, those most near to us in time, to the era of Leo XIII, and to those Latin Secretaries who, like A. Volpini, C. Nocella, V. Tarozzi, A. Angelini, A. Galli, and others, knew how to compose the most important documents with classical dignity and decorum, and through whom the Supreme Pontiff communicated to the bishops, the priests, and the people of the whole Catholic world his teachings and his exhortations as universal shepherd of the Church. This is a difficult and delicate job that requires great and long preparation and more than the ordinary amount of talent. And it is for this reason that, today especially, on the occasion of the Second Vatican Council, it is necessary to double the ranks of good Latinists and give them a complete formation. This formation is made more difficult not only because of that indifference and superficiality that all lament, but also because the technical terms, which have increased in number on account of the enormous advances in the natural sciences and on account of the new problems that modern thought and life pose uninterruptedly, can cause the translator to become the traitor by engendering confusion in those places where precision and accuracy are absolutely necessary.

I have complete confidence that Latin, this language which, to quote Pliny the Elder, *tot populorum discordes ferasque linguas ser-*

monis commercio contraxit, has united with community of speech the discordant and barbarous languages of so many peoples (*Historia Naturalis* III, 6, 2), this language which first cemented the union of so many nations in the vast structure of the Roman Empire, and which later on, through the work of the Church, served to bring together as brothers in the one great family of the *civitas christiana* all the barbarian peoples who had broken in from every direction, may once again serve as a strong instrument of communication, and be not only a bond of unity in the Church, but also a bond of unity among nations.

Through this bond of linguistic unity, all nations, divided by ideologies, disputes, and languages, will see the superiority of Rome, of which Ovid long ago wrote: *Gentibus est aliis tellus data limite certa: Romanae spatium est Urbis et orbis idem*; the territory allotted to other nations has definite limits, but the whole world is the domain of the City of Rome (*Fasti* II, 683-684).

VII
Latin and Esperanto

1. CAN LATIN REALLY BECOME AN INTERNATIONAL LANGUAGE?

When my *Italian-Latin Dictionary of Modern and Difficult-to-Translate Words* first came off the press, some Esperantists thought that, having enriched Latin with new terms and having thereby accommodated it to modern times, I was planning thereby to supplant Esperanto. Nothing could be further from the truth.

With the goal of making my intentions clear and of defining accurately the terms of the question that was being discussed in various publications, even foreign ones, I decided to express my views in print.

I am a devoted student of Latin, but not a fanatic. I will say right off that if one means by international language something that is understood and spoken by all the peoples of the world, then the question was settled long ago when, after the fall of the Roman Empire, the different national tongues slowly came into being, which, both in popular usage and in literature, supplanted the ancient imperial tongue of Rome; each nation wanted to have, and indeed ended up having, its own language.

Latin, therefore, was an international language only while it was imposed by the conquering power; it came as the colonizer and bringer of Roman civilization, at first enriched with the Greek heritage, and later strengthened by Christian thought. When the Empire fell and the whole human race was broken up into different ethnic and linguistic entities, it was inevitable that, at least among the people, the use of Latin would be supplanted by that of the different vulgar tongues.

We are therefore dealing with an historical problem which has now been settled in the most absolute manner possible. Petrarch was still unsure about this in his time, and he decided to entrust his literary fame to his Latin poem *Africa* rather than to his Italian *Canzoniere*, but Dante saw further, and after having begun *The Divine Comedy* in the language of Vergil, foreseeing the new times to come and the new linguistic developments among the people, he composed his greatest poem in the new language, which was sprouting like a vigorous shoot from the old Latin trunk.

Then there came the humanists, who gave a new life and a new impulse to the old language of Rome, and who composed pages worthy of the century of Augustus. But the people did not understand them, and their writings, however wonderful, were valued only in the restricted circle of the learned and the cultured. There was also a school of thought among the humanists that tried to suffocate and suppress the vulgar tongues, then everywhere rising, and replace them with the one imperial language supported and sustained by the Germanic Holy Roman Empire, Latin.

But history could not turn back; Latin was then and remains today the language only of the learned and cultured, nothing more.

Then, when the natural sciences and technology made those enormous advances, which we all so admire today, even many scientists thought it necessary to free themselves of the ancient tongue of Rome, which they considered incapable of expressing new subjects and the innumerable new inventions. Thus, for example, Galileo, having written his *Sidereus Nuntius* in Latin in 1610, so that all the scientists of the world might understand him, later on set aside this language, then common to all the learned men of his age, and began to compose his works in Italian, a novelty for which Kepler severely rebuked him, calling it "a crime of contempt for humanity."

People still continued to write in Latin, it is true, in medicine, anatomy, botany, and zoology, for example, C. Linneo, G. M. Lancisi, G. B. Morgagni, M. Malpighi, and not a few others. Right up to the most recent times, one still wrote medical prescriptions in Latin, in North America until around 1831, in Spain until about 1865, in Sweden until around 1872, in Germany until about 1882, and in Austria until around 1882, and some doctors still do so today.

But by this time one could say that Latin had been left to men of

Latin and Esperanto

letters and humanists; scientists resolutely abandoned the ancient language of Rome, each in favor of his own native tongue.

This was certainly a great calamity, because it broke apart that linguistic bond by means of which researchers in every part of the world could take notice, through this one language, of whatever scientific genius and progress had produced in the field of human learning.

Nevertheless, it is my opinion that it would be ridiculous to propose that Latin be made the international language of all peoples.

No one can claim that people learn Latin well enough to understand it and speak it properly, even if we mean Mediaeval Latin instead of Classical Latin. It would be absurd to imagine that the tourists who come to Italy might be able to speak in Latin with the inn keepers, with the taxi drivers, or with the tour guides that confront them at the entrances to the basilicas and the other monuments of Rome, and one would have to say the same thing with respect to other cities and other nations.

Ought one then to look for some other language which might be the common link to hold together all peoples and all nations?

Many have thought so and have made truly praiseworthy efforts in this direction. The desire to provide a common linguistic bond to our divided world is certainly a most noble one. If everyone spoke the same tongue, it would without a doubt be easier to understand one another, and this would remove many causes of misunderstandings, ambiguities, and disputes.

But, I wonder, is it really possible today to impose a single international language upon peoples linguistically divided among themselves?

Once Latin, the linguistic cement of a great but now fallen empire, had been abandoned, some thought of another, national, language to replace it, French, for example, or English. But this will never happen, because no nation would permit a foreign tongue to displace its own language, if only for reasons of pride and prestige.

In the case of Latin, this consideration of national pride and prestige was not felt, because Latin was considered, as it still is today, far above and beyond all feeling of nationalism.

Once Latin was set aside, and every other modern language likewise rejected, some thought that the only possible solution was to create an artificial language that everyone could accept without any question of race or nation popping up, a language which would at the same time express every thought, every result, and every discovery of science and progress.

2. ESPERANTO

Various attempts were made, but the only one that had noteworthy success was that of Dr. Louis Lazar Zamenhof, the author and creator of Esperanto. His intention and work were certainly noble and praiseworthy: to give divided humanity a single linguistic bond. I believe, however, that an artificial language can never be a true language. In order truly to deserve the name of language, it has to be something alive, something born from the mind, from the sensibility, and from the heart of a people, not from a formula or a mechanical calculator. Only if it can respond to the special genius of a people, to all the necessities expressed by the human heart, to all the different shades of thought, sentiments, and ideals, can it be and be called a language. A prefabricated language will always be something dead, and will, at best, be nothing more than one more language among many.

In saying this, I do not want in any way to belittle the lofty and noble goals that Dr. Zamenhof set for himself, and by which his successors are even today motivated.

When the Esperantists held a convention in Rome, they requested an audience with the Holy Father Pius x, who greeted them and blessed them as he greeted and blessed all his children and all those who wanted to draw near to him. From this, however, one cannot claim, and even less publish, as some have done, that St. Pius x approved of Esperanto as a universal language. This was not his intention, nor could it have been.

What is more, between Latin and Esperanto there has never been, nor could there ever be, antagonism of any sort, and this is for a very simple reason, namely, that Esperanto aspires to be an international language, whereas Latin does not.

Latin only wants to be the official language of the Church; what is more, it can and ought to be the common language of the learned. Even today, when Latin is in decline, there is in every country a reasonable number of people who know Latin and who are able to express themselves and their thoughts in it with various degrees of fluency. For most of them, this will not be the Classical Latin of Cicero, nor even that of our humanists; it will be that easier Latin that came into being in the Dark Ages and in the early Middle Ages when, the vulgar tongues not having yet developed, everyone still wrote in Latin. Or, perhaps, it might be the simple, clear, and flexible speech of our scholastic philosophers, or the so-called scientific Latin which our scientists, physicists, doctors, and anatomists used right up to the end of the eighteenth century.

Why should one not continue on this bright path, which might once again provide to all the learned of the world a common link?

Let no one say that this is impossible because Latin is too difficult and has too small a vocabulary. If it is too difficult, then one must study it harder, and if it has too small a vocabulary, then one must enrich it with the necessary new terms.

Two Necessary Steps

In my opinion, two steps are necessary before the language of Rome can recover the status it held as the linguistic channel of the learned right up to the end of the last century.

1. *First of all, a more practical method of teaching*

Today, unfortunately, many learn Latin as if it were a science instead of a language. There are too many syntactical subtleties, too much criticism, too much philology, but almost no practical training in writing and speaking in Latin. A lot of theory and no practice, and this is why the students in our schools are bored and hate Latin. They study it under compulsion until they pass their examinations; then they abandon it forever with a sigh of relief. Unless we change our method, it will always be like this.

2. *Enrich the Latin lexicon with the necessary new terms*

Let no one say that this is how one pollutes a language. Horace himself, in his *Ars Poetica*, allows for this, provided, of course, that one proceeds with the necessary restraint and prudence. What is more, this is precisely what our humanists did, our epigraphists, and many of our scientists, right up to the beginning of the last century. One can introduce new words and at the same time respect the native genius of the Latin language. Sometimes these will be short periphrastic expressions, useful for the most part for those who want to compose inscriptions and literary compositions, and on other occasions there will be a need for a technical term, to be derived *parce detorta* (with as little deviation as possible) from a Greek root or, by analogy, from expressions already existing.

The Example of the Church

To those who shrug their shoulders as if to say that it is an impossible dream to make Latin once again the linguistic bond among the learned, one can point to the example of the Church. In the Church, Latin is still today, as a matter of fact, the living and official language. The Church uses it today just as she used it in the past to transmit her teachings, her orders, and her wholesome admonitions to the whole Catholic world. She teaches in Latin today as she did yesterday; she legislates in Latin in the Roman Curia, in the Ecumenical Councils, and in the Synods. She gives her verdicts in Latin in her tribunals; she prays in Latin in her churches. The chief documents of the Roman Pontiffs, the encyclicals, bulls, briefs, and *motu proprios*, are ordinarily written in the ancient language of Rome. Let no one say that these documents have to be written in Latin because they deal with things of a bygone era and have nothing to do with modern life and thought. Whoever reads the *Acta Apostolicae Sedis*, the official organ of the Holy See, will immediately be convinced of the opposite. No one of those great problems that agitate today's world is absent from those pages, in so far as all of them, directly or indirectly, are related to the great religious and moral questions that lie at the base of human life. Philosophy, like theology, politics, like pedagogy, are examined there from the serene and penetrating viewpoint of the Gospel.

Not too long ago, for example, an encyclical of Pius xi, *Vigilanti Cura* (A.A.S. 1936, p. 249 ff.), looked into the motion picture indus-

Latin and Esperanto 85

try and did not have difficulty in expressing in the ancient language of Latium things and concepts that are typically modern. Some years later, norms and directives about an almost unknown science were given (A. A. S. 1942, p. 148), and, more recently, a whole encyclical of Pius XII, *Miranda Prorsus* (A. A. S. 1957, p. 768 ff.), treated expressly and in full detail all the issues involving motion pictures, radio, and television. What is more, the Roman Congregations, the chief ministries of the Church, usually write in Latin, and their teachings and directives are received and put into effect in all the extremities of the world. The Code of Canon Law is composed in Latin, and in the Roman ecclesiastical universities, as in schools in many other cities of Europe, Asia, and America, the teaching is ordinarily done in Latin, and just as the professors have no difficulty, when they lecture, in expressing themselves in Latin, scholastic Latin rather than Classical Latin though it may be, even when they have to deal with the most modern and various disciplines, so also the students follow the progress of the lectures comfortably and give evidence, in their drill sessions and papers, of their knowledge and cultural progress.

If, then, in the Catholic Church, the Latin language is still, after so many centuries and so many vicissitudes, the official language that unites peoples and nations spread out over the whole world in its capacity as the living and indispensable vehicle of the Supreme Magisterium, why cannot it once again, even in the great community of human thought and culture, become the universal instrument of communication among the learned? If the Church has overcome and continues to overcome all the difficulties that have arisen in using Latin, why would the great family of learned men of all nations not similarly be able to overcome them? Facts are more important than arguments, and the facts not only prove that a solution is possible, but they also point out the way to be taken, namely, the way which the Church has taken and continues to take. Even in the question of Latin, as in every other, she is moved by higher and universal motives.

The day on which the learned of the world, following at least in part the example of the Church, decide to learn how to use this common linguistic bond, if not for the complete texts of their books and papers, then at least for a summary placed at the beginning, a Latin summary that would give sufficient information about their thoughts and scientific discoveries even to those who do not know their own language, that day will mark a step forward in achieving mutual understanding among peoples and easier communication of the achievements of human culture and of the inventions of the human intellect.

VIII
The Latin Language Alive in the World

1. LATIN IN THE SCHOOL

Latin — Yes!, Latin — No!, Latin — How?
When the attack against Latin in Italy grew acrimonious, I felt compelled in conscience to express my opinion clearly. To the consternation, no doubt, of many, I did not align myself on the side of those who wanted Latin to be a required subject for everybody, for the simple reason that to me, Latin for everybody means wasted time for everybody. To the two sides *Latin — Yes!* and *Latin — No!*, I would like to add a third: *Latin — How?*

I believe that mandatory attendance at school for those 14 years of age and younger is a very just system of instruction, and it has been adopted, as a matter of fact, in other countries as well as ours. This means that everyone, even peasants and manual laborers, have the right to enough education to enable them to be good and free citizens, to understand the problems of life and society, to make their own intelligent and useful contributions, and to maintain a decent standard of living. Now what good is Latin for them? Or, to be more precise, one academic year of Latin? I think that it would be time lost, time that could be better spent on more useful matters. Latin is a serious subject.

If one can learn only a little in one year of studying a modern language, so, then, in studying Latin for only one year, there is only one thing that a student will learn, namely, how to grin and bear something worthless, because one year of Latin is useless, given the conditions of the majority of pupils, who cannot continue on with the subject.

One may then object that studying Latin causes discrimination by introducing an aristocratic element into education, insofar as only the children of the rich can continue school beyond the age of fourteen and thereby benefit from it.

To this I reply, first of all, that one can most efficaciously take care of this problem by setting aside scholarships for those poor students who have a true ability and disposition to continue their studies beyond the legal minimum; what is more, we should, I feel, arrange for suitable integrated studies, including a serious amount of Latin, for those who plan to progress from elementary school to high school and beyond. This is all the more necessary because if our youngsters are not able to choose their course of studies when they are eleven years old, they will with difficulty be able to do it at fourteen years of age, when mandatory schooling ends. A process of selection, and therefore of integration, is thus necessary.

Having one school for everybody does damage to everybody. It harms those who do not continue their studies because it lays down a foundation upon which they will never build anything; it will *begin* teaching them some things, like Latin, which will never amount to more than a useless and inconclusive smattering of knowledge for them, and they might more profitably have devoted their hours of study to matters that would have proven more practical and useful in their station of life.

Having only a common school for all would furthermore harm those who plan to advance further in their education, right up to the university, because, for these students, the three years of schooling that remain after they leave the common school but before they enroll in the university, the three years when their minds are fresh and supple and their memories most tenacious, these three years are not sufficient to provide the rigorous foundation for their future cultural progress, a foundation which must be laid right from their youth. This is particularly true in the case of Latin, which one has to study in earnest; it's one of those things one ought not to begin studying unless one intends to finish.

In my opinion, therefore, parallel to the required elementary school, there should also be instituted, right from the earliest years, another kind of school, which would lay solid and secure foundations for higher studies, a school whence the ruling class will issue, *a ruling class which is necessary in any political system*.

Latin, an irreplaceable element of our culture, will surely have a worthy place in this type of school.

It is Utopian to reduce to a common denominator the brains, temperaments, and aspirations of all citizens. Not all minds, not all temperaments, are equal. To reduce them to a common denominator is, as I have said, unnatural, and therefore impossible. Quite rightly did Horace write: *Naturam expellas furca, tamen usque recurret.* You may drive nature out with a pitch-fork, but it will soon return (*Epis.* 1, 10, 24). Along the same lines, a French proverb affirms: *Chassez le naturel; il revient au galop.* What's bred in the bone comes out in the flesh. Not everyone can be professors, doctors, engineers, or scientists. Those who think so are imagining a society more Utopian than that of Plato.

2. THE DEVELOPMENT OF LATIN INTO ITS CLASSICAL, PATRISTIC, MEDIAEVAL AND MODERN FORMS

I now conclude my observations on Latin with the ideas which I recently discussed in lectures in Florence, Montepulciano, Catania, Caserta, and Trieste.

The Roman tongue, that language which is perhaps the most logical, organic, and harmonious in the world, has twice received from Deity the historic mission to unite and cement nations together into a superior civilization and thereby become the vehicle of mutual communication and the bond of unity. This happened for the first time when the Roman legions, marching victorious to the extremities of the earth, created that empire of which Cicero said, *patrocinium orbis terrae verius quam imperium poterat nominari* (*De Officiis*, II, 8), it could more truly be called the support of the world, rather than an empire over the world, and which, according to Pliny the Elder, *tot populorum discordes ferasque linguas sermonis commercio contraxit* (*Historia Naturalis*, III, 6, 2), drew together through the fellowship of language the rude and various tongues of so many peoples. In this way was formed that universal community of nations of different races, which assimilated in itself by that one language all that was great, beautiful and true which the ancient civilizations, especially the Greek, had produced.

The second time was when, after the thousand-year old empire of the city of Rome had been overthrown by the barbarian hordes and the deep corruption of paganism, the thought, learning, and language of Rome, now become Christian, was enriched and spread everywhere by the monks, bishops and missionaries whom the Roman Pontiff was sending out along the old consular highways as unarmed messengers of truth to the Franks, the Britons, the Germans, the Batavians, the Frisians, and even to the unknown peoples of Slavonia, Scythia, and Tartary, so that one could say of Rome *quidquid non possidet armis, religione tenet* (Prosper of Aquitania, *Carmen de Ingratis* 41–44, in Migne, *Patrologia Latina* 51, 97), whatever she does not possess by arms, she rules by religion. With words not entirely free of rhetoric, but nonetheless very true, a great humanist, Lorenzo Valla, comparing the Roman Empire to its language, wrote:

> *De comparatione imperii sermonisque Romani hoc satis est dixisse. Illud iam pridem, tamquam ingratum onus, gentes nationesque abiecerunt; hunc omni nectare suaviorem, omni serico splendidiorem, omni auro gemmaque pretiosiorem putaverunt et quasi deum quendam e caelo demissum apud se retinuerunt. Magnum ergo latini sermonis sacramentum est, magnum profecto numen, qui apud peregrinos, apud barbaros, apud hostes, sancte ac religiose post tot saecula custoditur, ut non tam dolendum nobis Romanis, quam gaudendum sit atque ipso etiam orbe terrarum exaudiente gloriandum. Amisimus Romam, amisimus regnum atque dominatum . . . verumtamen per hunc splendidiorem dominatum in magna adhuc orbis parte regnamus* (In sex libros elegantiarum praefatio, I).

It is enough to have said this when speaking of the Roman Empire and of the Roman language. Peoples and nations cast off the one as if it were a disagreeable burden, but the other they prized as sweeter than nectar, more splendid than silk, and more precious than gold or any other gem, and they jealously maintained it as if it were something divine that had come down from heaven. And it is certainly true that the Latin language is an uncanny thing; great indeed is its divine power, for foreigners, barbarians, and enemies alike have preserved it fully and religiously for so many centuries that we Romans should not mourn but rejoice before the whole world. We lost Rome, we lost the Empire, we lost power... but nevertheless, by means of the more splendid influence of this language we continue to rule over a good part of the earth.

Now who is responsible for this immortality and universality of the Latin language? Certainly most of all the Catholic Church, which, making it its own, infused it, so to speak, with its own immortal, unifying and pacifying vitality, and used it to spread the Gospel, make all peoples brothers, and create a *Civitas christiana*.

In that great shipwreck of peoples, institutions, and civilizations that was the fall of the Roman Empire, as the genius and faith of the city were not entirely submerged, neither was its language. It is true that the emperors, the consuls, and the legionaries spoke no more, but above the immense ruins and raging deep, the Popes, bishops, and new apostles of the gentiles spoke aloud. The language of Latium, slowly transforming itself, continued to resound throughout the world and bring together new peoples, made brothers under the beneficial influence of Christianity.

Christian Latin

The first examples of Christian Latin were quite modest and without any literary pretense. They were generally translations from the Greek, written up in a simple way, clear but rough, quite close to the *sermo rusticus* or common speech already in use among the people. Such were, for example, the ancient versions of the Gospels, the Acts of the Apostles and the Letters of the Apostles, that is, the Letters of St. Paul, St. Peter, St. John, etc. But then there was felt the need to assimilate and to transfer into Christian thought whatever of beauty and literary perfection the language of Rome had produced in its great classical writers. That is, it was thought, and quite rightly, that art and literature could and should serve to illustrate and to propagate the precious religious and moral treasure which Christianity had brought to the earth.

The Apologists and Western Fathers, writing in Latin, provided a breath of new life for that ancient tongue which, with the decline of the Roman Empire, was itself deteriorating and becoming a bit barbarous; thus, in Tertullian, Cyprian, Minucius Felix, Ambrose, Jerome, Augustine and the two Popes Leo the Great and Gregory the Great, one found pages so beautiful and fresh that they compete with those of the authors of the Golden Age.

Later on, the Doctors of the Church and the Philosophers, especially the Scholastic Philosophers, created a Latin that was decadent as a literary form, to be sure, with respect to syntax and vocabulary, but more nimble, more flexible, and closer to the new way of thinking, brought back to life with the yeast of the Gospel and made mature from long meditations in the cloisters. At the same time, the *Studia Urbis* or *Studiorum Universitates* which had arisen in the principal towns were speaking, writing and educating in Latin. In the churches, one prayed in Latin, and in the Councils and Synods one even legislated in Latin. In a word, the whole life of the Church unrolled, developed, and progressed as she continually expanded, ever using that language as a universal medium and noble instrument to unite peoples and create the new Christian community.

Right up to the beginning of what is called the modern epoch, there is a lack of Pontifical documents that encourage the study and cult of Latin, for the simple reason that in those times it was not a controversial matter, and it was admitted by all that Latin was not only the official language of the Church but also the common tongue of the learned of every nation; it was therefore sufficient for the Church and for the Popes to emphasize the importance of Latin merely by using it, by practical example. There was also a time when certain humanists thought that they could supplant the vernacular languages, then rising and flourishing, with that one imperial language, Latin, which they wanted to make the single and universal language of the Holy Roman Empire.

The Humanists

When Charles v was elected emperor, Romulus Amaseus, an elegant Latinist and uncompromising Ciceronian, in his famous Latin address, did not hesitate to affirm most solemnly that only the ancient language of Rome was capable of expressing great thoughts, and that the vulgar, national languages were merely for the use of the mob. This was clearly an open and most grave exaggeration.

But no less grave and dangerous is the exaggeration of those people today who would like to reduce the teaching of Latin in the schools to zero (or something close to zero), condemning it as a useless burden which should be replaced by more interesting subjects of a utilitarian sort, more appropriate for modern life and activity. Today, that is, some people are planning to make school elementary and technical, leveling the culture of the young not by lifting those on the bottom up, but by pushing those on the top down, producing thereby a ridiculous equality of brains which, by natural law, are not and never can be equal, but must be treated each according to its own capacity, not evened out to some mediocrity that extinguishes all desire to be the best and to live up to the highest standards.

The first group of whom I have just spoken, those who think like the humanist Romulus Amaseus, go against the sovereign requirements of the new peoples; in order to conserve intact the glorious trunk of Latin, they propose to lop off the shoots that spring from it, shoots which Dante, Shakespeare, Victor Hugo and Goethe have given us. The second group, on the other hand, in order to give greater life to and provide more room for development of these linguistic and literary shoots, want to dig out the deep roots whence these draw their lifeblood. The former, in a word, were dreamers, who wanted to turn the clock back; the latter are superficial technicians who know no better than to prefer reinforced concrete to poetry, technology to thought, and machines to art, and who do not understand that without the classical languages, our culture would be an edifice constructed on quicksand, an improvisation that, taking no account of the past, would not be able to survive into the future.

The history of civilization, like that of culture, does not develop by leaps, without continuity; rather, it is like a series of blocks piled one upon the other. Woe is he who removes the first block, for the whole pile will then come crashing down into the abyss, an abyss that will lead to a new form of barbarism, albeit with a veneer of civilization.

The Work and the Influence of the Church

The Church has always avoided both the extremes of which I spoke above; she allows and favors the new national languages, but she wants, at the same time, to have a universal language for all, namely, her own official language, Latin, which no truly educated person can ignore, and which can serve as a bond of unity for her great international community.

If, as I have already pointed out, one can rarely find the call and exhortation to study Latin in the Pontifical and Conciliar documents of old times, precisely because the need was not felt to do so, it is nevertheless true that the Church, and in particular the Popes, have always rendered good service in this respect.

Who, we may ask, saved whatever remains of Latin literature from universal barbarism and illiteracy if not the Church? When, at the time of the barbarian invasions, everything was sacked, destroyed, burned and forgotten, the Popes, the bishops, and the monks tried to save the masterpieces and precious documents of Roman and Christian literature.

While the gale winds were destroying everything that ancient civilization had imagined and constructed, the Popes, the bishops, and the abbots of both big and small monasteries were forming libraries where the ancient codices were jealously guarded and which the quiet and hard-working monks transcribed and often illustrated with precious miniatures. In this regard Leo XIII, in his Pontifical letter *Plane Quidem* addressed to the Cardinal Vicar of Rome on May 20, 1885, correctly observed:

> *Hoc summum beneficium Ecclesiae debetur, quod libros veteres poetarum, oratorum, historicorum latinos graecosque magnam partem ab interitu vindicavit. Et, quod nemo unus ignorat, quibus temporibus bonae litterae vel per incultum et neglegentiam iacerent, vel per armorum strep-*

itus Europa tota conticescerent; in communibus monachorum ac presbyterorum domiciliis unum nactae sunt ex tanta illa turba barbariaque refugium.

The Church performed this supreme service: she saved from destruction a great part of the old books of poets, orators and historians, both Latin and Greek. And furthermore, as everyone knows, while literature lay prostrate because of ignorance and neglect or indeed altogether ceased throughout Europe on account of the din of battle, it found its only refuge from this commotion and barbarism in the monasteries of the monks and the residences of the priests.

For this reason, the word *cleric* came to mean *literate*, because churchmen alone kept lit the flames of knowledge and art amidst the darkness round about them.

Not only was the ancient patrimony of Roman thought and literature saved, at least in great measure, but in the Church one continued to write in Latin. Even in the darkest period of the Middle Ages, the Roman Pontiffs published all their documents in Latin. There was thus formed in the Roman Curia a style of writing with its own special rules, the *Stilus Curiae Romanae*, which had so great an influence on all the chanceries of Europe and which was taken for a model by almost all the Latin authors of the time. It was not a classical Latin; this new Latin, which flourished in the Middle Ages, diligently prized, more than purity of literary form, syntax, and vocabulary, the *cursus* (the flow of discourse), the *clausula* (the close of a period), and the rhythmic or metrical cadences.

The masters of the *ars dictandi* (the art of composition) who had their hub at the Roman Curia and whose patrons were the Popes, codified the subtle and accurate norms which had to be followed in Latin composition. These norms, which were supposed to be held secret, reached such a level of precision that one was able through them to distinguish forgeries from the authentic Pontifical documents truly written at the Roman Curia.

Once one gets beneath a surface which is, from a literary point of view, sometimes rough and harsh, the Roman Chancery prose of the Middle Ages, on account of the aforementioned norms or *dictamenta*, achieved a singular harmony and musicality. During the eleventh century, this Latin of the Chancery underwent a great development and revival, and it contributed not only to the rebirth of Latin letters and culture, but also to the formation of the various national languages, which at that time were everywhere in a state of germination. (See *Traduzione e poesia nella prosa di arte italiana dalla latinità medioevale a G. Boccaccio* by Alfredo Schiaffini, Genoa, 1934.)

Quite rightly did Augusto Conti write in his *History of Philosophy*, speaking of Thomas Aquinas, that his Latin, and indeed mediaeval Latin in general, was the womb of the new Romance languages, for it gave them that looseness and limpidity which distinguish them from the ancient classics.

The Humanists and the Church

The rules on which the style of the Roman Curia and a great part of mediaeval Latin prose were modelled are discussed by Pietro Fedele in the preface of the volume of Francesco Di Capua, *Fonti ed esempi per lo studio dello Stilus Curiae Romanae medievale*, Loescher & Co., Roma, 1941, pp. III–VIII. Of fundamental importance in this subject is the work in three volumes by the same Francesco Di Capua, *Il ritmo prosaico nelle lettere dei papi e nei documenti della Cancelleria Romana dal IV al XIV secolo*, the Lateran University, Rome, 1937–1939.

When, at the end of the fourteenth and the beginning of the fifteenth century, there arose that artistic and literary movement that we are accustomed to call humanism, one no longer paid attention just to the subtle rules and periods of the ancient rhetoricians and the *magistri artis dictandi* (teachers of the art of composition) but aspired most of all to renew Latin letters according to the ancient classical models, giving them a new breath of life, so that Latin became classical once again, albeit enlivened with the thought of the new times.

Everyone knows how the Popes fully favored this humanistic movement and how some were themselves humanists, so that Rome became the center of this reflourishing of Latin letters. Leo XIII wrote in his Pontifical letter *Plane quidem* of May 20, 1885:

> *Neque praetereundum, quod ex Romanis Pontificibus Decessoribus Nostris plures numerantur clari scientia harum ingenuarum atrium, quas qui tenent eruditi vocantur. Quo nomine permansura profecto memoria est Damasi, Leonis Gregoriique Magnorum, Zachariae, Sylvestri II, Gregorii IX, Nicolai V, Leonis X, Eugenii IV. Et in tam longo Pontificum ordine vix reperiatur, cui non debeant litterae plurimum. Providentia enim munificentiaque illorum, cupidae litterarum iuventuti passim scholae et collegia constituta: bibliothecae alendis ingeniis paratae . . .*

Nor must it be overlooked that of our predecessors the Roman pontiffs, many are deemed illustrious in the knowledge of those noble arts the professors of which are called *learned*. In this number, surely of lasting memory are Damasus, Leo the Great, Gregory the Great, Zachary, Sylvester II, Gregory IX, Nicholas V, Leo X, and Eugenius IV. And even in such a long list of Pontiffs, there is scarcely one to whom literature does not owe much. For by their foresight and generosity, schools and colleges were founded far and wide for young people eager to study literature, and libraries were prepared to sustain the learned.

As a result, even the *Stilus Curiae Romanae* was profoundly modified and transformed. Filippo Bonamici, the elegant Latin secretary of Clement XIV (1769–1774), wrote a book entitled *De claris pontificiarum epistolarum scriptoribus* (Noteworthy Composers of Pontifical Letters) in which he not only listed the papal Latinists from St. Jerome's time to his own, but also indicated, with wisdom and the proper discernment, what the style of the Pontifical Latin

Secretaries ought to be. They should, he said, avoid two extremes, each equally blameworthy. One extreme is that followed by people such as Aonio Paleario, Giulio Scaligero, and especially Pietro Cardinal Bembo, all of whom, on account of their love of classical Latin, expunged from their vocabularies all those new words which were necessary for the expression of the dogmas of the Christian religion, words which the Fathers and Doctors of the Church had wisely derived from the profane classical authors according to the laws of semasiology and semantics. (Bonamici wrote, on page 41 of his work mentioned above, "*Valde peccatum est ab iis, qui veterum Latinorum verba ita cupide atque intemperanter amplexi sunt, ut alia omnia fastidirent, atque illa etiam quae aut necessitas asciverat, aut religio consecraverat.*" Surely they have erred who have so fanatically and excessively embraced the vocabulary of the old Latinists that they eschew all other words, even those required by necessity or adopted by the Church.) For example, they called the Holy Trinity *triforme numen*, the Virgin of Loreto was *dea lauretana*, and the Pope they spoke of in the following way: *creatum fuisse Pontificem beneficio deorum immortalium, ac Iovis veluti personam gerere* (he who was made Pontiff through the favor of the immortal gods and who, so to speak, takes the place of Jove himself). On this subject, another elegant humanist, Antonio Muretto (1526–1585), correctly wrote:

> *Ne illorum stultitiam imiteris, qui usque eo antiquitatis studiosi sunt, ut voces quoque christianae religionis proprias refugiant et in earum locum alias substituant, quarum nonnullae etiam impietatem olent; qui non* fidem sed persuasionem; *non* sacramentum corporis dominici, sed sanctificum crustulum, *non* excommunicare, sed diris devovere, *non* Angelos sed genios; *non* baptizare, sed abluere *dicunt, aliaque eodem modo depravant; qui, ut opinor, nisi sibi metuerent, etiam pro Christo* Iovem Optimum Maximum *dicerent. Est enim magis Ciceronianum.*
> (Variarum Liber xv, I)
>
> Do not imitate the foolishness of those who are so fanatical about antiquity that they spurn even those

words that are proper to the Christian religion and substitute others in their place, some of which smack of impiety. For example, they say not *faith*, but *persuasion*; not the *sacrament of the body of the Lord*, but the *sanctifying loaf*; not *excommunicate*, but *make over to the Furies*; not *Angels*, but *Guardian Spirits*; not *baptize*, but *cleanse*. Other words they distort in the same way. They would even, I think, if they did not fear for themselves, go so far as to call Christ *Jupiter, the Best and the Greatest*, for that would be more in the style of Cicero.

Another elegant humanist, Mariano Prathenio (1712–1786), has rendered a similar verdict in his *Commentarii de vita et studiis Hieronymi Lagomarsini*, on pages 151–152. Against the extremists there stands the golden classical and yet Christian Latin of Sadoleto and many others, such as Andrea Rapiccio, Bishop of Trieste, who flourished as an elegant poet in the beginning of the sixteenth century.

The other grave error to be avoided is that of those who, in the words of the aforementioned Filippo Bonamici, propose that the Latin of the Fathers and of the Roman Curia should abandon all classical elegance and accept into its lexicon without discrimination every word coined in the time of bad Latin and even of the worst Latin, which policy would result in a barbarous and variegated hybrid that would be more to the disgrace than to the honor of the Church.

Of these people, thus writes the forenamed Latin secretary of Clement XIV:

> *Qui omni prophanorum contempta elegantia,* ecclesiastice, *ut ipsi aiunt, scribi dicunt oportere, ... si nulla puri sermonis, nulla numeri habita ratione, tertio quoque verbo ingerant* filialem *oboedientiam,* paternum *zelum, aliaque huiusmodi; si sacris e libris verba utcumque inferciant, et sensus quosdam afferent mutilos atque hiantes, eamque ob causam germanos se esse scriptores ecclesiasticos, ne illi egregie falluntur; et quam vereor, ne in hac ecclesiastici*

styli quasi latebra eorum delitescat inscitia. Fuga enim laboris, qui est in recte scribendo sane maximus, disertam (quod ait Cicero) neglegentiam reddidit imperitorum; ut id non oportere disputant, quod propter ignaviam non libet. (Filippo Bonamici, *op. cit.*, 43–44. These same ideas were expressed in elegant Latin by the famous humanist Giacomo Facciolati (d. 1769), the teacher of the outstanding lexicographer Edigio Forcellini. See *Iacobi Facciolati Orationes, Oratio* III, *p. 69 s., Typis Seminarii, Padua, 1774*.)

Those who hold in contempt all the refinement of the profane authors say that they must write, as they put it, in the *ecclesiastical* style. If they care nothing for unadulterated language, if they do not pay attention to rhythm, if every third word in their bloated sentences is *filial* obedience, or paternal *zeal*, and other things like that, if they stuff their works with all sorts of words taken from the Bible and produce crippled and poorly constructed sentences, then their defense is (if it is not simply a matter of their having grievously blundered) that they are true ecclesiastical writers, and under this pretext of Church Latin, I fear, there lurks gross ignorance. For they avoid hard work, which is indispensable if you want to write properly, and this avoidance is the cause of the eloquent carelessness (as Cicero says) of these ignorant fellows, for they claim that what they, on account of their laziness, are incapable of doing is anyway unnecessary.

Under the aegis and patronage of the Roman Pontiffs, we have had a whole series of Latin writers who have made the language of Rome resound with renewed dignity in the documents of the Church; this they did by avoiding both traps, that is, the trap of repudiating those Latin words which Christianity has consecrated as absolutely necessary to express Catholic doctrine, and the trap of falling into slovenliness, barbarism, and the unpolished style of dilettantes.

The Principles of the Church in Her Use of Latin

This seems to be the right place to set straight a matter which certain people handled incorrectly in the past. The matter is: What type of Latin is it that the Church proclaims as her official language and which in fact still is her official language in the liturgy, in her principal documents, in her Councils, in her Synods, and in the daily lectures at her major schools?

The Church accepts and favors with every means at its disposal ancient, classical Latin, which is the true literary language and of which there are the most noble traditions in the great Pontifical documents, that is, in the Encyclicals, the Consistorial Allocutions, and the Apostolic Letters. However, she does not want to ignore, let alone reject, that age-old Latin which the learned have been forming and transforming over the centuries as a result of new needs and the new developments in human thought inspired by the stimulus of Christianity. For the Church, Latin is not a dead language, but a live one; it is not merely an object of erudition and of study according to the great classical models, but is also an instrument of communication and a bond of unity. For this reason, she allows, in addition to Classical Latin, the Ecclesiastical Latin of the Fathers, the Doctors, and the liturgy, as well as that more nimble, more tractable, more flexible, and easier form that we are accustomed to call Scholastic Latin.

I shall therefore say that these criteria of universality, even in the matter of the Latin language, are the real reason why that language has never died in the life of the Church. If the Church, in fact, had closed herself up in the ivory tower of Ciceronian Latin and had excluded from her use that age-old Latin that took form later on in response to the needs of the new times, she would with difficulty have been able to maintain throughout the manifold range of her activities the living use of that language.

I believe therefore, that here at last is the secret why, after so many centuries, the Church still keeps her official language alive, namely, she has embraced and continues to embrace Latin in all its manifold and glorious history, and, according to the different circumstances, needs, and stations of her people, she has used and continues to use this universal language in the form most appropriate to her purpose and to the level of education of the people whom she is addressing.

The Church is a great international, and therefore supranational, society; her official language cannot therefore be that of a single nation but must have the genius of that universality that transcends every boundary and avoids and happily overcomes every possible rivalry for pre-eminence or prestige among the different peoples.

A Constitution on Latin

In conformity with these traditions, the late Pontiff John XXIII published the Apostolic Constitution *Veterum Sapientia* in defense of Latin in general and especially to give a new impetus to the study of that language, particularly in the seminaries, ecclesiastical schools, and universities of the Catholic world.

The noble summons of the Pope was accorded a great and resounding reception such as usually greets a major historical event.

The need for this Constitution was felt especially by those who viewed with sadness the decline of Latin particularly in our Italy, the chief heir of the glories of Rome and of its harmonious, precise, and soundly constructed language which twice, as I have pointed out, has united and made brothers out of the world's peoples in a higher civilization, and which even today is not only the necessary and fundamental basis of our culture, but also the official and still living language of a great supranational society, the Catholic Church, which consists of 500,000,000 faithful spread throughout every extremity of the earth and speaking so many different languages.

I certainly do not want to claim, as I have said before, that the ancient language of Rome should be a new Esperanto to serve the common people; that would be to return to the fantastic dream of Romulus Amaseus. I intend instead to affirm that Latin, if studied in the same way that our humanists studied it, can once again be the vehicle of thought among the educated and a bond of unity among all peoples.

In the great Ecumenical Council, the ancient language of Latium has once again become the *unitatis mirabile vinculum* (the wonderful bond of unity). And mark this well; this one language, whose sounds have echoed under the vault built by Michelangelo for the great basilica, has not proven to be merely a spectacular symbol of the unity of the Church but has furthermore served to express, with that precision which the vulgar languages, on account of their constant evolution and transformation, cannot approach, those incontrovertible truths of Catholic dogma which the language of the Holy Fathers, the Councils, and the Roman Pontiffs has consecrated in unequivocal terms in accordance with a more than millennial tradition.

In this respect, a French scholar, G. Bardy, in his book *La question des langues dans l'Église ancienne*, rightly notes that one of the principal reasons for the Great Schism between the East and the West was the two different languages they used, for after the fifth century, the Greeks no longer understood the Latins, and the Latins no longer understood the Greeks, and even the famous German historian Anton Michel similarly observes, "The ignorance of the other's language (for language is the key to the spiritual life of a people) contributed, to a certain extent, to the Schism between the East and the West, whereas sharing a common tongue would have helped lessen or at least weaken the forces that were working for separation... The whole world of the Latin Fathers remained hidden from the Greeks... and the West was incapable of offering its works to the East." (See *Sprache und Schisma*, in *Festschrift Kardinal Faulhaber zum achzigsten Geburtstag*, München, 1949, p. 68.)

In this way, neither side understood the other in the subtle discussions of dogma, and the Great Eastern Schism was the result.

Great prudence must be used in allowing other languages, especially in the liturgy, lest that of which Sallust complained once again be proven true. *Nos vera vocabula rerum amisimus* (*Catilina*, c. 52), we don't have the right words for these things any more, and equivocation, uncertainty, and quibbling fatally work their way into the most sacred and immutable matters.

The Debate about Latin

The Apostolic Constitution *Veterum Sapientia* does not deal with Latin merely as the official language of the Church, but also exalts its importance as the foundation of culture and the instrument of education in our schools. The Constitution uses the following firm and wise words with respect to the efficacious formative power of Latin:

> No one can call into question the quite special efficacy which the Latin language and, more generally, humanistic culture have in developing and forming the tender minds of the young. Latin, in fact, cultivates, ripens, and perfects the best powers of the spirit, it promotes agility of mind and adroitness in rendering judgment, it enlarges and consolidates young minds so that they learn how to come to grips with and evaluate things properly, and, finally, it teaches one to think and speak with consummate precision.

This solemn affirmation of the supreme ecclesiastical authority, accompanied as it was by sound provisions for the establishment of a school for the study of the best Latin to be inaugurated in Rome, appeared to some to be like a blast from one of those large-mouthed guns that are fired to disperse hail-storms, a blast fired against dense clouds that had, for several years, been spanning the horizon and threatening to wipe out or at least upset the teaching of Latin; others, however, those who hate Latin because they are ignorant of it or have no more than a superficial knowledge of it, those to whom it brings back memories of yawning at their school desk, and especially people who loathe Latin because it is the language of the Church, these others have cried foul and have claimed that we are returning to the Middle Ages and are putting a useless burden on the backs of our children. All of these people are products of the transformation of modern culture accomplished by technology, machines, supersonic jets, and interplanetary voyages, things, they say, that are useful and not the mere dreams of poets.

Let me give an example. In the newspaper *l'Unità* of March 2, 1962, they dare to say that the Vatican, in issuing this new document, is trying to stage a comeback of "this cold, fossil of a language... which cannot contribute anything to the education of our youth". One need only point out that only a few months before, the famous Russian philosopher Borovski, in a lecture delivered in polished Latin at the University of Leningrad, had recommended the promotion of the language of Rome, which he called the best teacher there is of arts and letters (*litterarum et artium optima magistra*) and a language that can make an incalculable contribution to the most weighty cause of a more liberal education of the people (*ad gravissimam illam causam liberalioris institutionis publicae*).

How do we explain this contrast between the learned Russian professor and the newspaper quoted above? It is quite simple; it is a lack of solid culture, or at least gross levity and superficiality that makes one call the language of Cicero, Vergil, Julius Caesar, and so many others a "cold language" that has nothing to teach our youth.

I would like, moreover, to mention here one aspect of Latin, or rather a reason for its importance, that appears to me to be of the greatest significance but which few nevertheless have examined in sufficient depth. The Latin language is not only the official language of the Church but is also the fundamental substratum of our civilization, a substratum upon which many wonderful things in the arts and sciences can be constructed, according to the culture and genius of the various nations, but which no people can do without. Let me explain. The vernacular languages of today reflect the particular genius of each people and often provide quite a contrast when compared one with the other; they are the mirror and the image of different nationalities and different civilizations in continual evolution. However, the ancient language and culture of Rome reflect the SYNTHESIS of different civilizations and combine them into a unity; into it there flows, as if into a marvelous melting-pot, the thought of the greatest thinkers whom mankind has ever produced, along a route that takes us from the nations of the Orient, through Egypt and Greece, all the way to the shores of the Tiber. Along this route, their thought has been enriched by all the elements of the human soul and has reached such heights and universality that one should call it the thought not of one people but of the whole human race. It is the eternal and universal basis of humanism which is now the common inheritance of all peoples and which no single people can ignore.

Rome, having inherited the wisdom and art of Greece, used its genius to make them universal and adapt them for all minds, so that one can say, with Pius XI in his document *Officiorum omnium*, that in the designs of Divine Providence, Latin became a worthy instrument to perform that supernatural grafting of the divine onto the human which was brought about by Christianity. This grafting is represented architecturally by the arch, which was unknown to the Greeks but invented by the Romans, the arch between the divine and the human; Latin literature became such an arch, as Tertullian, alluding to the pagan authors of the classical age, pointed out: *O testimonium animae naturaliter christianae* (*Apologeticum* XVII, 6), these writings are evidence that the human soul is by nature Christian.

In the aforementioned document *Officiorum omnium*, Pius XI spoke of Latin as

> *Hoc... loquendi genus pressum, locuples, numerosum, maiestatis plenum et dignitatis, quod mire dixeris comparatum ad serviendum Romani Pontificatus gloriae, ad quem ipsa Imperii sedes tamquam hereditate pervenerit.*
>
> This concise, rich, and melodious way of speaking, full of grandeur and merit, which was marvelously ready and waiting, you could say, to serve the glory of the Roman pontificate, to which the very seat of the empire devolved as if by inheritance.

No people, therefore, can be jealous of Rome, because Rome belongs to the whole world; no people can be jealous or envious of the Latin language, because she is, or rather ought to be, the language of all learned men.

The Reasons for the Decline in the Study of Latin

It is an undeniable fact that today the study of Latin is in sharp decline among us, and, in my opinion, there are two main reasons for this.

The first, which applies to everybody, is this: modern civilization is the civilization of the machine, the civilization of technology;

whatever does not produce, that is, whatever is not useful and thus utilitarian, is therefore no longer of interest and is abandoned or at least left to those few who still live in the stratosphere of literary ideals and who, to the present generation, appear to be no better than grave diggers who are trying to unload a useless burden, a corpse, on the backs of our youngsters.

But these criteria would lead to the banishment not only of Latin, but of all the eternal values of the human spirit. Civilization would flatten out, become materialistic, and lose its soul; reinforced concrete, as I have said, would be worth more than poetry, the motion picture industry more than Vergil, and the atomic bomb more than the dome of Michelangelo.

For this reason, perhaps, some people today do not dare to banish Latin entirely but instead, with premeditated calculation, cautiously try to reduce the study of it in order later on slowly to suffocate it; this is surely a more insidious plan than the former one.

The second principal cause for the decay in the study of Latin is, in my opinion, the sterile emphasis on theory by certain zealous professors, who do not understand the proper place for their scholarship.

The ideas I am going to express on this point are inspired by the teachings and exhortations on the study of Latin by the Sovereign Pontiffs, and they especially and fully conform to what has been set forth in the Apostolic Constitution *Veterum Sapientia* of John XXIII and the *Motu Proprio* of the reigning Pontiff Paul VI, *Studia latinitatis*, wherein he implemented the constitution of his predecessor by founding at Rome an international Pontifical Institute, *Latinitas*. In the aforementioned *Motu Proprio*, after having recommended "a better knowledge of both ancient and recent Latin," it is set down that "the teaching of Latin should be accompanied and sustained by constant practice in writing Latin, so that the pupils not only arrive at a solid knowledge of the Latin tongue, but also learn how to write in it efficiently, purely, and with taste." By these words, it is clear, it is recommended that the practical and humanistic method of teaching Latin be employed, and not just that sterile theoretical method that reeks of erudition, which makes learning Latin an odious chore for the young.

Today, alas, in many schools, one teaches more theory and scholarship than Latin; that is to say, in the early grades one teaches just grammar, consisting ordinarily of the old stereotyped systems according to the formula *ex libris libri fiunt* (make new books out of old books), and in the higher grades and universities, a lot of philology, textual criticism, and aesthetics. These things are all very useful, and a good instructor can easily put on quite a show, while the pupils wearily doze off or stare at the ceiling.

The educational system in vogue today is INSTRUCTIVE, but it is not CONSTRUCTIVE. One must remember and keep in mind that Latin is really not a SCIENCE, but a LANGUAGE. One must therefore learn not only to understand it but also to enjoy it, to write it, and to speak it; otherwise, one misses the very purpose of a language.

The teacher who limits himself to scholarship (even if quite vast) is like a fellow who dissects a corpse, all the while pointing out the precise function of each of the organs, or to a mechanic who dismantles an automobile, indicating as he goes along the purpose of each part; then it all ends, the corpse remaining a corpse and the machine remaining a heap of inert parts.

It is necessary to give movement and life to one's teaching, and this can be accomplished by adding Latin composition to what would otherwise be lifeless grammatical rules, requiring the students to express their thoughts, their feelings, and the things they see, hear, and taste in the ancient language of Rome.

Latin needs a renewal, not of its morphology and syntax, but in thought, in content, and consequently in a good deal of its lexicon, namely, in that part of it that must express all that is new in the thought and attitudes of modern life. Our humanists did this, and we shall have to do it as well if we want to promote the revival of this language, which is the root stock of our own national language, Italian, a language which we shall never be able to understand fully right down to its depths and in all its colorations if we are ignorant of Latin.

It is necessary, in conclusion, to return to the humanistic method of teaching Latin if we want the students to get interested in it, and if we want it to flourish once again in our schools.

At this point, I should like to quote the following important words of the poet Giacomo Zanella (1820–1888), which sound as if they were written today:

> Once upon a time, it used to be the special boast of the Italians that they wrote Latin better than any other European people; indeed, many of our writers of the sixteenth century, such as Fracastoro, Vida, M. Flaminio, G. Casa, B. Castiglione, and Ludovico Ariosto himself were not far behind the authors of the Golden Age of Augustus... Foscolo was in contempt of the decree of the Cisalpine Republic, which tried to abolish the study of Latin in the schools... The way Latin is taught today will bring us to the same end that was feared and lamented by Foscolo. Since linguistics prevailed over aesthetics, and the minute analysis of a single word over the artistic observation of the thought, Latin in our schools became an empty waste of time; indeed, the young do not lose an hour to forget it all as soon as they get to the university.

The Ministers of Public Instruction, Ferdinando Martini in 1891 and Guido Baccelli on November 10, 1894 (both of them were not only Ministers of Public Instruction but also Latinists and humanists), issued admonitions in this regard that those in high places would do well to consider even today. The latter, Guido Baccelli, in a circular letter on the study of Latin in the schools, used these words:

> The children will not learn to love that divine language, yea, they will learn to hate it, if there, in the school, they find the teacher all too ready to bore them and terrify them with the dryness and intricacy of grammatical rules.

This will happen all the more if those same teachers, he said, do not bring the subject to life by the living use of the language. The former minister, Ferdinando Martini, gave his assent to a statement of the Commission for the Teaching of Latin that went like this:

In the grammar schools, grammar has cast its long shadow over the immortal flowers of ancient thought and covered them with a cloud. The youngster leaves school and throws his books away, Vergil, Horace, Livy, Tacitus! Every line in them, one could say, was a trap that hid a grammatical snare for him, cost him so much work, and brought on so much yawning.

After these stern warnings that we should return to the humanistic method of teaching Latin, warnings which have, in substance, been wisely repeated in the Apostolic Constitution *Veterum Sapientia*, I have nothing more to say except to recall the observation of the great Greek historian Plutarch, who wrote, "The minds of the young are not vases to fill but torches to set aflame!" What is needed therefore is not to stuff the brains of our children with sterile theoretical rules, but to light the torch of true Latinity.

CONCLUSION

The patient reader, having arrived at this point, will have noticed, so he thinks, that this book consists of two different parts, the first of reminiscences of my time as Secretary of Letters *ad Principes*, and the second an impassioned defense of Latin in life and school.

One can spend one's life in grand human enterprises; circumstances — and for this I give thanks to Providence — caused me to choose the simple and compelling road of service to the Latin language, faithfully accomplished at the side of great men who, through the language of Rome, taught and continue to teach the truths that are a comfort and a hope for mankind.

For the rest, the articles I have written and the speeches I have delivered for the defense and increase of the Latin language are no more than a reflection and, I would say, an obligation of my position, forty years in duration, in the office of the Latin Secretariat of the Pope, where I drew up the most important Pontifical documents.

Anyone who has written in Latin for such a long period of time and on the gravest questions and problems that he is used to thinking in Latin (even through a Tuscan) would at the same time feel the duty to defend the glorious language of our ancestors, neglected today as it is and even the object of plots in our very midst, in the midst of us who are the most direct heirs of this noble cultural tradition.

INDEX

Acta Apostolicae Sedis, 17, 74, 84
Acta Leonis, 46
Acts of the Apostles, 91
Ad Petri Cathedram, 59
Africa, 80
Ambrose, St. (circa 340–397), 92
Angelini, Achille (1812–1889), 76
Aquinas, Thomas (1225–1274), 96
Ariosto, Ludovico (1474–1533), 109
Ars Poetica, 47, 83
Augustine, St. (354–430), 92

Baccelli, Guido (1830–1916), 109
Bardy, Gustave (1881–1955), 103
Bartolini, Msgr. R., Florentine who accompanied Bacci to the Vatican, 4
Bembo, Pietro Cardinal (1470–1547), 75, 98
Benedict XV (1854–1922, reigned 1914–1922), 14, 33, 51, 70
Bisleti, Gaetano Cardinal (1856–1937), 74
Bonamici, Filippo Maria (1705–1780), 97, 98, 99, 100
Borovski, twentieth-century Russian philosopher, 105
Bridget, St. (circa 1303–1373), 68
Buonarroti, Michelangelo (1475–1564), 103, 107

Caccia Dominioni, Camillo Cardinal (1877–1946), 37

Caesar, Julius (100 B.C.–44 B.C.), 105
Cameriere partecipante, 18, 19
Canzoniere, 80
Carbone, Vincenzo, editor of Dehon, *Diario del Concilio Vaticano I*, 67
Cardinal, The (movie), 35–37
Casa, Giovanni della (1503–1561), 109
Caserta, 89
Castiglione, Baldassarre (1478–1529), 109
Catania, 89
Catholic Action, 27, 34
Charles V, Holy Roman Emperor (1500–1558), 93
Chrysostom, St. John (died 407), 57
Cicero (106 B.C.–43 B.C.), xvi, 69, 73, 74, 75, 76, 83, 99, 100, 105
Ciceronian, 93, 98, 101
Cisalpine Republic, 109
Clement XIV (1705–1774, reigned 1769–1774), 97, 99
Conti, Augusto (1822–1905), 96
Cortile della Pigna, 19
Cyprian, St. (210–258), 92

Damasus, Pope (366–384), 4, 97
Dante (1265–1321), 80, 93
Dehon, Léon-Gustave (1843–1925), 67–69
Di Capua, Francesco (1879–1957), 96
Divine Comedy, The, 80
Dubois, Louis-Ernest Cardinal (1856–1929), 74

Esperanto, 79-86, 102
Eugenius IV (1383-1447,
   reigned 1431-1447), 97

Facciolati, Giacomo (1682-1769), 100
Fasti, 77
Fedele, Pietro (1873-1943), 96
Flaminio, Marcus Antonius
   (*circa* 1498-1550), 109
Florence, xv, 1, 2, 3, 4, 73
Florence, Council of, 73
Folengo, Teofilo (1491-1544), 47
Forcellini, Egidio (1688-1768), 100
Foscolo, Ugo (1778-1827), 109
Fracastoro, Girolamo
   (1483-1553), 109

Galilei, Galileo (1564-1642), 80
Galli, Aurelio Cardinal
   (1866-1929), 76
Garibaldi Monument, 19-24
Georges' *Latin-German Lexicon*, 44
Goethe, Johann Wolfgang von
   (1749-1832), 93
Gospels, 91
Gregory the Great (*circa* 540-604,
   reigned 590-604), 92, 97
Gregory IX (reigned 1227-1241), 97

Holy Roman Empire, 80, 92
Holy Year, 34
Horace (65 B.C.-8 B.C.),
   47, 83, 89, 110
Hugo, Victor (1801-1885), 93

*Italian-Latin Dictionary of Difficult-
   to-Translate Words*, xiii, xvi, 43-47
Italy, 16, 30, 34, 63, 81, 87, 102

Janiculum Hill, 19-24
Jerome, St. (347-*circa* 420), 4, 92, 97
John the Evangelist, St., 91
John XXIII (1881-1963, reigned 1958-
   1963), 55-62, 63, 64, 65, 67, 102, 107
Jubilee, 16, 34, 52

Kepler, Johannes (1571-1630), 80

Lancisi, Giovanni Maria
   (1654-1720), 80
Lateran Pacts, 16, 21, 26, 27
Latinitas, xiii, 46, 107
Leo the Great (*circa* 400-461,
   reigned 440-461), 41, 92, 97
Leo X (1476-1521, reigned
   1513-1521), 97
Leo XIII (1810-1903, reigned
   1878-1903), 19, 20, 23, 24,
   26, 44, 75, 76, 94, 97
Leonine Walls, 21, 24
Letters of the Apostles, 91
Linnaeus, Carl Nilsson
   (1707-1778), 80
Livy (59 B.C.-17 A.D.), 110

Malmantine, 3
Malpighi, Marcello (1628-1694), 80
Martini, Ferdinando (1841-1928), 109
Mater et Magistra, 59
Meditazioni 59
Mermillod, Gaspard Cardinal
   (1824-1892), 69
Michel, Anton (1884-1958), 103
Migne, Jacques Paul (1800-1875), 90
Minucius Felix (second and
   third centuries A.D.), 92
Minutante, 9

Index

Miranda Prorsus, 46, 85
Mirandola, Pico della
  (1463–1494), 45
Mistrangelo, Alfonso Cardinal
  (1852–1930), xv, 3
Mit Brennender Sorge, 27
Montepulciano, 89
Montini, Giovanni Battista.
  See Paul VI.
Monza, 32
Morcelli, Stefano Antonio
  (1737–1821), 47
Morgagni, Giovanni Battista
  (1682–1771), 80
Muretto, Antonio (1526–1585), 98
Mussolini, Benito (1883–1945), 27, 35

Nicholas V (1397–1455,
  reigned 1447–1455), 97
Nocella, Carlo (1826–1908), 76
Non Abbiamo Bisogno, 27
Non expedit, 16

Officiorum Omnium, 106
Oratio de Eligendo Pontifice, 35, 56
L'Osservatore Romano, 28, 71
Ottaviani, Alfredo Cardinal
  (1890–1979), xvii, 63
Ovid (43 B.C.–18 A.D.), 77

Pacelli, Eugenio. See Pius XII.
Pacem in Terris, 59
Palaestra Latina, 46
Paleario, Aonio (1503–1570), 98
Papini, Giovanni (1881–1956), 15
Passavalli, Archbishop Luigi
  (1821–1897), 73
Paul, St., 76, 91

Paul VI (1897–1978, reigned 1963–
  1978), xix, 4–6, 15, 16, 63–66, 107
Penitentiary, Apostolic, 14
Peter, St., 15, 19, 21, 25, 36, 43,
  51, 61, 64, 66, 67, 91
Petrarch (1304–1374), 79
Pian habit, 17
Pie, Louis-Édouard François Desiré
  Cardinal (1815–1880), 69
Pignatelli di Belmonte, Gennaro
  Granito Cardinal (1851–1948), 35
Pius IX (1792–1878, reigned
  1846–1878), 19, 20, 21, 23, 24, 52
Pius XI (1857–1939, reigned 1922–
  1939), 15–34, 46, 51, 70, 74, 106
Pius XII (1876–1958, reigned
  1939–1958), 16, 35–54, 55, 56
Pizzardo, Giuseppe Cardinal
  (1877–1970), 5, 6
Plane Quidem, 94, 97
Plato (circa 428 B.C.–circa
  348 B.C.), 89
Pliny the Elder (23–79), 76, 89
Plutarch (circa 46–circa 127), 110
Pogiani, Giulio Cardinal
  (1522–1568), 75
Ponzano Romano, 13, 15
Prathenio, Mariano (1712–1786), 99
Prosper of Aquitania (circa
  390–circa 463), 90

Ragazzoni, Archbishop
  Gerolamo (1537–1592), 73
Rapiccio, Andrea (1533–1573), 99
Ratti, Achille. See Pius XI.
Renzo, fictional character in
  Manzoni's I Promessi Sposi, 47
Robinson, Henry Morton
  (1898–1961), 35

Romulus Amaseus (1489–1552), 93, 102
Roncalli, Angelo Giuseppe. See John XXIII.
Sadoleto, Jacopo Cardinal (1477–1547), 75, 76, 99
Sallust (86 B.C.-*circa* 35 B.C.), 71, 103
Scaligero, Giulio Cesare (1484–1558), 98
Schiaffini Alfredo (1895–1971), 96
Schiassi, Filippo (1763–1844), 47
Sebastiani, Nicola (1866 or 1867–1931), xv, 9–15
Sedia gestatoria, 27
Sidereus Nuntius, 80
Spada, Msgr. Domenico, Chancellor of Apostolic Briefs from 1922 to 1949, 5
St. Peter's Basilica, 16, 36, 37, 56
Studia Latinitatis, xix, 107
Stilus Curiae Romanae, 95, 96
Sylvester II (*circa* 946–1003, reigned 999–1003), 97

Tacitus (*circa* 55-*circa* 120), 9, 14, 110
Tardini, Domenico Cardinal (1888–1961), 42, 71
Tarozzi, Vincenzo (1849–1918), 76
Tertullian (*circa* 155-*circa* 230), 92, 106
Theresa of the Child Jesus, St. (1873–1897), 25, 26
Trent, Council of, 60, 73, 75
Trieste, 89, 99

Valla, Lorenzo (1407–1457), 90
Vatican Council, First, 23, 60, 67, 69, 70, 73
Vatican Council, Second, xv, xvi, 25, 60, 67, 69, 70, 76
Vatican Gardens, 21, 24, 47
Vatican Polyglot Press, 18, 67
Vergil (70 B.C.-19 B.C.), xvi
Veterum Sapientia, xix, 67, 102, 103, 107, 110
Vigilanti Cura, 46, 84
Vida, Marco Girolamo (*circa* 1485–1566), 109
Volpini, Alessandro (1844–1903), 76

World War I, 1, 33
World War II, 38, 51

Zachary, Pope (reigned 741–752), 97
Zamenhof, Louis Lazar (1859–1917), 82
Zanella, Giacomo (1820–1888), 109

ABOUT THE TRANSLATOR

Anthony Lo Bello is Professor of Mathematics at Allegheny College, Meadville, Pennsylvania. He received his A. B. degree from Kenyon College in 1969 and his Ph.D. degree from Yale University in 1975. He is the author of several books, among which are *The Commentary of Albertus Magnus on Book I of Euclid's Elements of Geometry* (Brill Academic Publishers, Inc., 2003), *Origins of Mathematical Words: A Comprehensive Dictionary of Latin, Greek, and Arabic Roots* (Johns Hopkins University Press, 2013), and *Origins of Catholic Words: A Discursive Dictionary* (Catholic University of America Press, 2020).

Also available from
AROUCA PRESS

Meditations For Each Day
Antonio Cardinal Bacci

Integrity, Volume 2
The Second Year (January – June 1947)
Edited by Carol Robinson & Ed Willock

The Pearl of Great Price:
Pius VI & the Sack of Rome
Christian Browne

Liberalism:
A Critique of Its Basic
Principles and Various Forms
Louis Cardinal Billot, S.J.
(Newly translated by Thomas Storck)

Understanding Marriage & Family:
A Catholic Perspective
Sebastian Walshe, O. Praem.

www.ingramcontent.com/pod-product-compliance
Lightning Source LLC
Chambersburg PA
CBHW070913080526
44589CB00013B/1282